Why
You're
Not
Married...
Yet

BALLANTINE BOOKS ☗ NEW YORK

Why
You're Not
Married...

The Straight
Talk You Need
to Get the
Relationship
You Deserve

Tracy McMillan

Copyright © 2012 by Eleven Thousand Lakes, Inc.

All rights reserved.

Published in the United States by Ballantine Books,
an imprint of The Random House Publishing Group,
a division of Random House, Inc., New York.

BALLANTINE and colophon are registered trademarks
of Random House, Inc.

This work is based on "Why You're Not Married"
by Tracy McMillan, which appeared in
The Huffington Post in February 2011.

LIBRARY OF CONGRESS CATALOGING-IN-PUBLICATION DATA

McMillan, Tracy.
Why you're not married—yet : the straight talk you need to
get the relationship you deserve / Tracy McMillan.
p.   cm.
   ISBN 978-0-345-53292-3 (hardcover : alk. paper) —
ISBN 978-0-345-53293-0 (ebook)
1. Marriage—Psychological aspects.   2. Self-realization.
I. Title.
   HQ734.M1816 2012
   155.2—dc23   2012009597

Printed in the United States of America on acid-free paper

www.ballantinebooks.com

9 8 7 6 5 4 3 2 1

First Edition

Book design by Debbie Glasserman

Contents

Quiz

Or, 38 Reasons You Might Need This Book

Answer as honestly as you can. If you're not sure, tell yourself you're fine and skip to the next question.

True or False

1. Sometimes I wonder what the big deal is about being in a relationship anyway.
2. My favorite thing to do is to *be right.*
3. I really want to be loved for who I am.
4. I'm at work so much, I've thought about painting my cubicle.
5. Nice people bug the shit out of me.
6. I have more than two godchildren. (Add 1 point for each additional godchild.)
7. Looks don't really matter, unless a guy is poor or stupid.
8. I have an advanced degree in a subject where there's no job at the end.
9. I've never cheated on anyone, ever—except for that one time.

10. As far as childbearing goes, my age falls somewhere between DGAF and OMFG.

11. Men fall in love through their woo-hoos.

12. I have snooped through a man's cell phone or computer.

13. I have forwarded myself emails or texts from a man's cell phone or computer. (Add 3 points.)

14. I have showed up unannounced at a man's place of business.

15. I sometimes wonder how they built the Great Wall of China with absolutely none of my input.

16. I've been told I'm needy. Which was bullshit.

17. I have broken up with someone by text message or voice mail.

18. I have looked at a man's picture on the Internet and seriously felt that I was going to marry him. (If you actually *did* marry him, add 10 points.)

19. I'm pretty sure I'm psychic.

20. If you add it all up, I've been in therapy for more than five years.

21. I subscribe to *Us Weekly*. (*In Touch*, add 5 points. *O*, add 8 points.)

22. I have a behavior or habit that I swear I will stop doing as soon as my husband shows up.

23. Letting go is overrated. I like to hang on to things.

24. I like to date guys with better jobs, faces, or families than mine.

25. Sometimes I think I'm fat/ugly/stupid—but I *don't* have low self-esteem.

26. My bookshelf is filled with self-help.

27. I've read *Twilight*. (If you finished it, add 3 points. If you

bought tickets for the movie ahead of time, add 7 points.
If you camped out in line, add 23 points.)

28. I've tried to do the "Single Ladies" dance at least once.
29. I find out a guy's astrology sign within the first week.
30. I know what zabasearch.com is.
31. I've sent a guy a cute email, text, or stuffed animal inside a coffee mug—even when, technically, we weren't dating.
32. My dad was a liar, cheater, gambler, criminal, and/or meanie.
33. My mom was a drinker, depressive, rager, gorgeous, and/or extremely well dressed.
34. My siblings were better-looking, smarter, more athletic, and/or the type of people who like to lord shit over you.
35. The family dog was a humper or had other psychological problems.
36. I have names picked out for my children. (If it's Bella or Edward, add 12 points.)
37. I'm single and I can't figure out why.
38. Marriage is stupid. And men suck.

Add Up Your Score

One point for each "True" answer, plus any extra points as indicated. Don't cheat.

1-9 POINTS: YOU SORT OF NEED THIS BOOK

But you'll be pretty sure you already know everything in it. So read it really quick, then do your single best friend, sister, frenemy, or co-worker a favor and buy another copy for her. Tell her you totally think it's bullshit, but it was just so stupid you had to give it to her. Suggest that when she's done reading it you guys can get together and laugh about how wrong it was. Cross your fingers that she'll end up learning something anyway.

10–19 POINTS: YOU NEED THIS BOOK
In the medical world, there's fine fine, and then there's fine-but-you're-going-to-have-to-take-care-of-that-thing fine. You're the latter. It's not that you'll *never* find a happy relationship if you don't figure out what's going on with you; it's just that you'll find it so much quicker if you do. And like a fungus, the longer you wait, the worse it gets. You just need to know exactly which type(s) of fungus you're dealing with. And by the time you're done reading this book, you will.

20–29 POINTS: YOU TOTALLY NEED THIS BOOK
Your love life is like New Year's Eve at the end of a really eaty, smoky, drinky year. You are *exhausted.* No one's denying you had some fun out there, but you are relieved the year is over so you can finally make some resolutions and get busy breaking them. For you, this book is like January 1—a chance to start over, and this time do it *right.* And if you're worried about falling off the wagon, don't. Because what you will learn in this book is that you *are* the wagon.

30+ POINTS: YOU REALLY, REALLY, *REALLY* NEED THIS BOOK
You already know something in your love life isn't working. What you didn't know is that *nothing* in your love life is working. But don't despair. Working on it is going to be a lot easier and more enjoyable than what you're doing now, which is trying to stay in denial. That shit is *hard.*

Introduction

ALL THROUGH YOUR TWENTIES, YOU WERE FINE—working, shopping, getting drunk on the weekends, and having sex with your boyfriend (or whomever), not necessarily in that order. Then something happened. Another birthday, maybe. A breakup. Your best friend's wedding. Suddenly there you were: walking down the aisle wearing something halfway decent from J. Crew that you would totally be able to repurpose with a cute pair of boots and a jean jacket. And as you made your way toward the altar, looking at a groom who wasn't yours (not that you'd even want that particular groom), you found yourself, for the first time ever, having something—*feelings?*—about the craziest thing:

Why you're not married. Why you're not even *close.*

Intellectually, you know there's nothing wrong with not being married, but then why does it feel kinda like there is? As if the Life Train is getting ready to pull out of the station and somehow you're stuck trying to buy a ticket at a malfunctioning kiosk. You keep swiping your credit card, but nothing happens. You're starting to wonder if this is like Europe, where your card needs to be embedded with some sort of magical chip to work.

The whole purpose of this book is to help you do something that—if you're like a lot of women I know—might pain you to even admit that you want to do. And that something is *get married.*

But let's get one thing clear right away. This is not a book about finding a man. In fact, it's hardly about men at all. Because getting married—as you've probably figured out by now—is not about finding a man. There are zillions of guys out there. The question is, how come you're not marrying any of them?

This is a book about *you.* About what kind of woman you are. Specifically, whether you are the kind of woman who is ready for marriage. And if you're not, how you can be. Naturally, you probably think you already *are* that woman. Who wouldn't think that? But one of the ideas behind this book is that you could probably stand to take a good, honest look at where you are—okay, a *gooder, honester* look—to really assess what your negative traits might be and how they might be holding you back. It's unlikely that you're doing every single thing wrong. But it's also unlikely that you're doing everything right. Only by being willing to really search your soul and look with compassion upon whatever you find there will you expand as a person—and, as a result, become ready (or more ready) for marriage.

The premise here is that marriage is about *love.* Not the kind of love where you feel like you're starring in a really amazing Banana Republic commercial. The kind where you take a risk, put your ego aside, let down your defenses, and decide to love a man for *who he is,* not what you want from him—even if what you want from him is to love him. (And, of course, marriage and a baby.)

It's as simple as this: If you're not married and you want to be, you need to *express* more love. Not *get* more love. Express it. Feel it. Be it. See it everywhere.

Like Madonna said—and I know this is cheesy—it's about opening your heart.

Gold Rings and Handguns

So who am I and why should you listen to me? Well, first off, I'm not the kind of expert who did everything right in relationships and is now going to pass along some golden tablets with the get-married info on them. On the contrary. I am a (formerly) royal mess when it comes to relationships—but I've worked my ass off to have a healing. Kind of a girl version of Robert Downey Jr.—if men were crack and gold rings were handguns—who finally hit rock bottom.

For the past ten years or so I've been a sort of combination lay therapist, love coach, and mating-not-dating sponsor. My "practice" takes place at the water cooler, in the cafeteria, at the coffeehouse, or in the ladies' room—usually when I'm supposed to be doing my real job. (I'm a television and film writer, and before that, I wrote broadcast news for fifteen years.)

Not that I ever went out seeking "clients." It's more like I delved into all sorts of different subject matter as a way of evolving *myself* (I totally needed evolving), and invariably I would find myself passing along what I had learned—mixed with my insights about people and my experiences in relationships. As the years went by, almost to my surprise, I started helping people. I'll never forget the time I was walking through a big mall in Beverly Hills and I ran into a girl I was acquainted with. She excitedly stopped me and told me that she'd taken something from a really nice chance conversation we'd had at a coffee shop two years earlier and now she was living with a great guy whom she loved. How cool! I was really happy for her and glad to know that I had contributed something to the planet in some small way. (The gist of that coffee shop conversation became what is now Chapter 9.)

That was the first of many such encounters. Since then, I've helped numerous women get on the road to marriage—usually not because I showed them how to get a guy, but because I helped them shift their perspective about being a woman. That changed how they thought about themselves and moved through the world, and the next thing you know they were walking down the aisle.

I'm also the mother of a teenage boy. I've said in the past, and I'll say it again, that fourteen-year-old boys are like the single-cell protozoan version of a husband. I often want to invite my single girlfriends over to my house for a day so they can get a clear picture of what they're really dealing with when it comes to men. It's not that all men are immature. It's that all men have a part inside them that matches the part inside me that never really left ninth grade. And in order to love them (and love myself), I'm going to need to get realistic about that part.

Then there's the other big thing about me: I've been married—and divorced—three times. (Yes, three.) Once each in the 1980s, 1990s, and 2000s. Somehow I also managed to squeeze in three live-in boyfriends and four less-significant significant others, plus pine after scores of unavailable men who couldn't or wouldn't love me. I was a busy gal.

In my decades of dating (and marrying) I have screwed up so many right relationships and chased after so many wrong ones that I've learned a lot about what works and what doesn't. Now I'm like a jailhouse lawyer who's done so much work on her own case that I can help you with yours. I know what you're doing wrong because I've done it. And I'm the first to admit that I've got a pretty dubious track record when it comes to staying married.

Getting married, however—*that* is a different story. Don't ask me why, but attracting guys who are willing to marry me—or are at least willing to cohabit—is like my main superpower. (Talking a lot is a very close second.) I've thought about this quite a bit and have come to the conclusion that while I am sweet and faithful, and a man can be sure he will never ever be bored with me, there's nothing particularly special about me. There are girls out there who are way more marriageable than me but who haven't seen a third of my action.

I think my success in this area is more about my readiness to move toward, and choose, men who are willing to make commitments. As well as—and this is *super* important, and often more difficult—the willingness to let go of the men who aren't.

I don't take full credit for this. A big part has to do with the fact that I grew up in foster homes. I entered the world of dating with one objective: to avoid men who would abandon me. If we were talking about presidents of the United States, I was all about gentle, thoughtful, lusting-only-in-his-heart Jimmy Carter—the Bill Clintons of the world could go blow their saxes in some other chick's bed. In my mind, the only thing worse than dating a guy like that would be marrying him, and I was all about getting married.

Let me stop right here. I bet you're wondering how I ended up walking down the aisle multiple times before plucking out a single gray hair. A lot of people assume I married bad men and/or am bitter about marriage as a result of my three divorces. Neither is the case. Here's the quick rundown.

HUSBAND #1. The second guy I ever slept with, a guy I started dating at age seventeen (to his credit, I lied; he thought I was nineteen) and wedded (on a boat) after a very reasonable two-year courtship. He was ten years older, with an MBA and a great job at a Fortune 500 company (where he *still* works, BTW, twenty-eight years later)—in other words, an honest-to-goodness great guy from a great family. The only problem was . . . me. I was just too young to make, and keep, that kind of commitment.

HUSBAND #2. Thirteen years later, along came Dan, a very nice minister's son I met at work. Six months into our relationship, at age thirty-one, I found myself pregnant. Wanting desperately to have the kind of family I dreamed of as a child, I knew what to do—commit—but I had no idea how to do it. Unable to surmount a lifetime of abandonment programming, after three years of marriage I just did what came naturally: I left. Okay, I only moved three miles away, but still. I simply could not tolerate the kind of closeness that comes with marriage to a stable, loving man. This is not an excuse; it's simply a fact. We are now candidates for the co-parenting hall of fame, or we would be, if there was one.

HUSBAND #3. Last but not least, there was Paul, whom I married at forty and divorced at forty-one. This was the guy I had been looking for my whole life—I was, in a word, *wildly* attracted to him—and what I found out is that sometimes "soul mate" is just another term for "gonna trigger all your deepest childhood wounds." I didn't know it, but Paul had all the best (and worst) qualities of my father—a guy for whom womanizing was more than a hobby, it was a vocation. About eight months into our marriage, Paul decided to start dating a twenty-one-year-old girl, so wisely I asked him to move out. It was a painful, painful period in my life—for both me and my son—but in that very special (and excruciating) way in which life tends to work, going through that relationship set me free. And I do mean *free*.

After spending entire relationships haunted by my desire for a certain kind of man—exciting, sexy, and yes, seriously unavailable—I know now firsthand what my version of Mr. Big was all about: anguish. In fact, my chief complaint about *Sex and the City* is that it made a relationship with Big seem desirable or even feasible, when in fact a fantasy man is just that: a fantasy. Ask any drug addict: trying to escape reality day in and day out is not only time-consuming, it's *agonizing*. Otherwise, dude, we'd all be doing it.

In short, my marriages "failed"—actually, "collapsed" is a better word—for one very simple reason: I wasn't yet the right woman for marriage.

Oh, So *That's* Why

Okay, so if you're still here, I want to welcome you to my funny, self-helpy, big-sistery, girlfriend-guide, spiritual-like, no-nonsense look at how to love more and love better. The principles in this book have the power to change your life. By the time you are done reading here, you will feel more hopeful than you have in years, because you will see that the stuff that's going on with you can be remedied if you're willing to deal with it.

There are ten chapters here—one for each of the big ways you might be sabotaging your ability to be in a relationship. I recommend simply reading the book once through with an open mind and heart. Then go back to a single chapter where you think you might have some work to do and spend a week just sort of living with the ideas in it. Practice making the suggested changes. Then move on to another chapter or area where you've identified a problem. Slowly you will incorporate these new ways of thinking about yourself when it comes to love and relationships. This isn't a sprint. It isn't even a marathon. It's a nice long walk on a crisp fall day. There might be some hills, but mostly you should just relax and enjoy it. This is the work of life.

Within each of these chapters, the basic issues at hand will be discussed first, such as what "You're a bitch" really means. Then I'll unwrap the headline to examine what I see as the core issue underneath, in the section called "What It's Really About." Each chapter will also include "Notes from My Life," which are special and not-so-special moments from my own life where I blew it in a similar manner to the way you may be blowing it right now. As well as a part called (for example) "Why Lisa's Not Married," so you can see how other perfectly nice women are screwing it up, too. This helps you see what you're doing—because you know how much easier it is to identify a problem when you're looking at it in someone else.

Every chapter will also cover "Some Relevant Stuff About Men," where I share with you what I've learned from men over the years. I think it helps to know that men usually aren't doing whatever they're doing *to* you; they're usually just doing it, and you simply happen to be in the vicinity. I've found that knowing this helps me to be not so mad at them.

After all that, we'll head into the solutions, with a section on "How You're Going to Have to Change," which will have nothing to do with wearing makeup, blowing out your hair, or loitering in the frozen foods section of the grocery store and other places where men congregate, but will have everything to do with *changing your mind*—about men, about marriage, about yourself. Then, because change is hard (if it wasn't, everybody would be doing it), we forge ahead to "Spiritual Stuff That Will Help You Change." This section will, as promised, put the problem in a spiritual context (don't worry, I won't go too woo-woo on you) and give you tools to help you actually make that change. Last but not least, we will wrap up each chapter with "What Your Best Friend [or Mom, or Co-Workers, or Ex-Boyfriend] Knows but Isn't Telling You," which is what the people who love you would tell you if only they had the balls. Instead you're hearing it from me, a stranger, though you will know enough embarrassing stuff about me by the end of this book that you will probably be judging me the way you do your closest friends. Which I hope means that you'll at least *consider* inviting me to your wedding.

Be forewarned: When all that's said and done, I'm going to suggest something completely punk rock. I'm going to suggest you get a *god*. Wait, come back. It doesn't have to be a bearded guy in the sky and a big church with a painted ceiling—but it needs to be *something*, anything, that isn't your mind or the stuff it's telling you. A place beyond reason and pure intellect. Because like I said, ultimately marriage is a spiritual trip. Even for chicks like you.

The bottom line is that marriage is just a long-term opportunity to practice loving someone even when you feel they don't necessarily deserve it. And loving is always spiritual in nature—because people are flawed and it's *hard* to love flaws. You can count on the fact that, most of the time, a man will not be doing what you want him to do. But because you are loving him anyway—because you have made up your mind to transform yourself into a person who is practicing being kind, deep, virtuous, truthful, giving, and, most of all, accepting of your own dear self—you'll find that you experience the very thing you wanted all along: love.

And I would not be at all surprised if you ended up married.

Why
You're
Not
Married...

1. You're a Bitch

Or, How Anger and Fear Are
Keeping You Single

1. Do people walk on eggshells around you—and you kind of like it?
2. Does the idea that you should be nice to a man make you angry?
3. Have past boyfriends felt that you were defensive or hard to get close to?

THE DEAL IS THIS: most men just want to marry someone who is nice to them. Nice includes sex, laughing, and occasionally—but not to the point of oppression or anything—cooking a meal, folding the laundry, or doing something else he's too lazy to do for himself. Just because you love him. That's what nice is.

Is this you? If my asking makes you mad, the answer is probably not.

But that alone doesn't make you a bitch. What makes you a bitch is that *you're mad at a guy for even wanting that stuff*. Being a bitch is about feeling superior to men (and the women who want them), rolling your eyes without even knowing you're doing it, and having a lot of tension around your mouth all the time. It's about radiating something that makes people feel just a little bit scared of you. And not only do you *not* care, but if you get really, really honest you would have to admit that you *like it.* Just a little.

That's being a bitch.

Bitch is less a personality characteristic than it is an *energy.* There's nothing wrong with it per se. We all have an inner bitch, and she is a powerful ally who protects us and keeps us from being exploited. But most of the time in relationships, as in life, you gotta keep your gun in your purse. Which is to say, there is a time and a place for your bitch—in a tough business negotiation, say, or when being threatened, but not on a dinner date. And not just because it's Thursday.

Unfortunately, bitch energy is distressingly common among single women. Maybe it's because somewhere along the way, being a bitch became synonymous with being modern. When I was coming of age, in the 1980s and 1990s, it was something to be proud of. There were even jokes that the word was an acronym for cute phrases like "babe in total control, honey" and "because I take charge here." Being a bitch was about claiming a place in the boardroom as well as the bedroom. It was a settling of old scores from all the years of male oppression. It was righteous. It was *empowering.*

But when it comes to dating and getting married (and, for that matter, being a mother), being in total control, honey, is an enormous liability. In fact, for most men—and women, too—it is an absolute deal breaker. Who in his or her right mind wants a mate who demands total control?

What It's Really About

So when I say you're a bitch, I mean *you're angry.* Now, you probably don't think you're angry. You think you're super smart, or—if you've been to a lot of therapy—that you're setting boundaries, or maybe that you're intellectually curious and like to debate a lot. But the truth is you're pissed. At your mom. At the pharmaceutical-industrial complex. At Sarah Palin. But perhaps most of all, you're mad at men. You're mad that they can hurt you, that they have the power to reject you, that they seem to want twenty-three-year-old ninnies over powerful and fabulous women such as yourself.

At least that's what you tell yourself. But my experience is, men don't mind powerful, and they don't mind fabulous. What they mind is emotionally unstable, annoying, scary, bitter, cold, and above all, *unloving*.

Female anger terrifies men. They won't come right out and tell you that, because half the time they don't even know it, at least not consciously. But after having a son, I now clearly see how much power a woman has in a man's life, and how our anger (and I'm not talking about pick-up-your-socks anger; I'm talking about baked-in, this-is-how-I-am-so-deal-with-it anger) affects them on a very deep level. To start with, every man has a mother, right? The same way we women have to deal with the template our fathers laid down for us in relationships, men have to deal with their mothers. Except times ten, because for the first several years of his life, that woman was the source of *everything* to him: love, frustration, scolding, cookies. There is no possible way to overestimate the impact of a man's mother on his psyche. Never mind his particular mother; I'm talking about the fact that he has one at all. And how about the fact that he *lived inside her body* at one time? Really. When you think about it, it's pretty crazy.

For this reason, we ladies need to be very conscious about how we express our anger. (Just as men should be conscious and caring about how they express theirs.) I know it seems unfair that you have to work around a man's fear and insecurity in order to get married—but actually it's perfect, since working around a man's fear and insecurity is a big part of what you'll be doing as a wife. And I don't mean this in a belittling way. It's the same thing if you want to be a mother—you're going to have to work around your children's fears and insecurities. If you want to be an employee, you're going to have to work around your boss's fear and insecurities. If you want to be a friend, you're going to have to . . .

Well, you get the picture. You're going to have to get a grip on your anger.

Notes from My Life as a Wife

At twenty, I was a young married bitch. People often say they know bitchy women who are married, and I can vouch for this, because I was one of them. But in my experience good marriages have a loving warmth and adoration between partners that is missing from the marriages of bitchy women. (As I'm sure it's also missing from the marriages of douchey men.)

It's not that I was all bad. I was a fun conversationalist, and I had a sense of adventure that generally kept things interesting. But I was also a person who didn't put a lot of boundaries around my own behavior. I disrespected other people while pretending to myself that I wasn't doing exactly that. I indulged the part of me that felt like she should be able to have the world look the way she wanted it to, even if it was at the (emotional) expense of other people.

In short, I was a bitch. And here's how I did it:

1. *I was controlling.* This is the number one weapon in the bitch arsenal. It's where you make sure nobody ever does anything that you don't like by preventing it in advance. And the way

Smile!

You know how they say men are visual creatures? Well, that doesn't just mean they prefer porn over erotica. It also means they pick up a ton of information about you *visually*. Which means—and this is going to sound weird, but it's important—*be aware of your facial expressions and body language*. Some of my bitchiest girlfriends have no idea of the look they're wearing on their faces. If they did, they would surely want to change it!

You have to think of your face and your demeanor as a visual expression of your inner thoughts and feelings. If you are habitually thinking angry, judgy, stressed thoughts, it is going to show on your face. It might surface as a really firm mouth, a hard look in the eyes, a curling lip, a habitual pulling gesture in the shoulder or arm, or any other bit of body language that might be saying something you don't mean.

Fortunately, there's a really easy place to start combating this: smile! And really mean it. Not only will it brighten the day of everyone around you, it will make you feel better, too. And it will make you a thousand times more attractive.

you prevent it in advance is by making everyone walk on eggshells. I would tense up my body the second anyone got near a topic I didn't like or started to do something I didn't like, then make faces (and sounds, if necessary) to communicate my displeasure. Anyone who stayed in my life past the first six months knew what this meant and backed off. Pretty soon the only people left were people who were going along with my program—which led me to assume that I was a perfectly agreeable young lady when, indeed, I was not.

2. *I was manipulative.* Being manipulative is the stealth way of making people do what you want while leaving no physical evidence behind. It involves things like talking "casually" to your mate about other people . . . while making it clear which of their behaviors you find reprehensible. Behaviors that, coincidentally, you have been badgering your mate about for the last day, week, or month, and would like him to stop doing *immediately.* If that doesn't work, there's also guilt and threats, where you just tell the other person that if they keep doing whatever they're doing that you don't like, you're going to either get cancer or leave them.

3. *I was judgmental.* My attitude was, "No one is doing anything right around here. Period." Also, I thought I was better than other people, which practically goes without saying. If you're like this, you know who you are.

4. *I was spiteful.* If you did something to me—or if I *perceived* that you did something to me—I wouldn't hesitate to retaliate. Getting back at you might come in the form of relentlessly pointing things out to you that you said yesterday, or cutting you down so you don't feel so confident, or (my personal favorite) teaching you a lesson. Ugh.

If that's not a list of traits someone would want in a wife, I don't know what is! Most of all, I had to be *right.* Because what I wanted more than anything else—even more than I wanted to be a loving person—was to dominate my husband. Which might sound irrational, but not really. I was afraid to be vulnerable. There was something about letting that one person, that *man,* have the power over me that goes along with being a husband that I just couldn't handle. Or, more accurately, I was going to handle it by donning a big pair of tall, shiny black boots and carrying a long dominatrix whip that I could snap whenever I felt like it. And when you think about how scared I was, it makes perfect sense that I behaved the way I did.

Why Leanne's Not Married

My friend Leanne has another form of the bitch problem, which manifests mainly through her extremely sharp tongue. She doesn't seem to understand that men are creatures who have feelings. I sometimes wish I could videotape Leanne and play it back to her, because Leanne's talking is more like another woman's ranting. Watching it, she might feel sick to her stomach for a while, but at least she would start to understand what's going on in her relationships with men and how they're experiencing her.

I'll never forget watching Leanne strike up a conversation in a restaurant once, with a very nice commercial director named Eric. I have an eye for guys who are willing to commit, and Eric was one of those guys. A little bit short, maybe, but so cute and nice. The fact that commercial directors make Mom-can-stay-at-home money is totally incidental as far as I am concerned, but it's the kind of thing Leanne cares about, so I was excited a cool guy seemed into her.

At the time, Leanne was really desperate to have a boyfriend, and really loath to admit it. She didn't want to be desperate. But at that point she'd been single so long, she'd begun to suspect there was something very wrong with her—something that was really obvious to other people, especially men. Most of the time this suspicion was too painful to confront head-on, so as an alternative, she convinced herself that she was too "intimidating" and "fabulous."

Anyway, Eric the director was telling us how he had recently directed a major beer spot and was editing it again on his own, because he didn't feel the client's version of the commercial represented his best work. "You mean," Leanne quipped cuttingly, "'Miller Lite: The Director's Cut'?" The smile evaporated from his face, the pleasure of sharing his work with her gone. She thought she was so smart.

What she was was dateless. Eric, who was obviously so interested at the beginning of the conversation, never even asked for her phone number.

Leanne doesn't know it, but her (all too common) defense is to reject men before they have a chance to reject her. Bitchiness is a mask for that fear—of being hurt, of intimacy. Leanne blames men for not liking her. "Men don't like me," she says. I can tell she enjoys the dubious look on people's faces. After all, she is a tall, striking brunette with a successful career as a corporate law-yer. Supposedly she's the dream—which just makes her doubly mad that she can't seem to get a second date.

It's as if Leanne is completely committed to a life where she is terribly misunderstood by men. What she doesn't grasp is that there is nothing wrong with *her,* but there is a lot wrong with the way she is behaving. It's unreasonable to expect to be a know-it-all, tell men all the stuff they're wrong about, snort derisively at their simplistic love of *South Park* and the *Sports Illustrated* swimsuit issue, be competitive with them, and then think that they are going to want to partner with you. Men are *people* first.

Some Relevant Stuff About Men

I often say that giving birth to someone's future husband has taught me everything I *really* needed to know about men. Like, here's what my teenager wants out of life: macaroni and cheese, a video game, and Kim Kardashian (or someone who could resemble her if you were squinting). Have you ever seen Kim Kardashian getting all intense and angry with a guy? I didn't think so. You've seen Kim Kardashian smile, wiggle, and make a sex tape. (And get married and divorced in less time than the rest of us take to pick up our clothes from the dry cleaners. But my kid doesn't know that.)

Don't get me wrong; I'm not saying you have to turn yourself into a male fantasy. You most certainly don't. (The type of guy who is willing to commit would probably pass on Kim, actually. She's a little too desperate for attention—I say that with all the love in my heart—and committing-type guys do not really want to deal with that.) I'm saying that inside every man is a very simple creature who just wants to enjoy a woman, not do battle with her. And you're not going to talk him out of it, even with a (perfectly valid) feminist argument.

But perhaps no single thing is going to cause a man to reject you the way bitchiness will. This is hard for many women to hear. They really want to make it about the man being insecure or misogynistic. Yes, there are some insecure and misogynistic men out there who want to retaliate for (and defend themselves against) the fact that women have the power to reject them. But honestly, that's just a male version of bitch!

There are other men, though—reasonable, good men—who see a bitchy woman and feel compassion. They can clearly understand that the bitchiness is coming from a place of hurt, yet they know they don't have the power to heal that hurt. So they don't even try. Because no matter how great a girl could be, no one wants to spend all his time, day in and day out, in the line of fire.

How You're Going to Have to Change

Which brings us to the nitty-gritty. If you're a bitch and you want to partner with someone, you're going to have to be different. The good news is, what you have to do is really, really simple. The bad news is, it will probably piss you off. So I'll just say it.

You're going to have to be nice.

Nice is the alternative to bitch energy. Men call this "sweet." If you ask a guy about the number one thing missing from women in the dating pool today, he will almost certainly tell you this: there is a major shortage of sweet women. And in the baccarat-like high-stakes world of marriage—which is a long way from the scratch-off lottery ticket excitement of dating—nice girls finish with a ring on their left hand.

So what is nice? First, let me tell you what nice is *not*. It's not being right most or all of the time, arguing about things a lot, having a really hard edge in your voice, focusing more on what a man doesn't have than on what he does have, or thinking men are picket fence delivery devices meant to give you children, support you, or complete some picture you have of your life.

Nice is soft, fun, kind, and, ahem, *penetrable*. Guys need to be able to get their thing into you. If you're too tough, they can't do that. A girl can be hot, sexy, powerful, smart, dynamic, and interesting, but if she's not sweet, most (not all, *most*) guys will not really want to marry her. He might be into the sex, dig your sharp wit, respect your job, and think you're a badass, but unless you add sweetness to the mix, those are just exciting destinations. Like, say, Reykjavik. It might be fun to visit, but the climate is too fierce for you to really want to live there. However, put Reykjavik in, say, California, and you've got a deal.

Check in with yourself right here. Did it just piss you off that a lot of men think nice is *sweet*? Does the idea of being sweet—or, more accurately, the idea of *having* to be sweet—make you mad? This is what I'm talking about. If it does, then you have a problem.

Being nice is not demeaning. It's what makes the effing world go around! And it's especially what makes a marriage work. It's called the Golden Rule, and as far as I'm concerned, it trumps everything. Unfortunately, one thing I notice about several women I know who are not married but would like to be is that they're not very nice, particularly to men. They don't treat men according to the Golden Rule because, at some level, they don't think they should have to. Even more commonly, they think they're nice but they really aren't. A good way to know if this is true about you is if, right now, you're super sure it isn't. Another way is to ask three of your closest friends if they think there's any chance people might perceive you as a bitch. If they give you one of those can-I-really-tell-her-the-truth three-second gazes, you have your answer.

Kindness is not something we place a big value on in our culture. We like snark, competition, and drama—at least to judge from the ratings for a lot of reality shows. Interestingly, a kind man is, we all agree, a good thing. No one has a problem asserting that a man *should* be kind. None of us would want our best friend to marry an unkind or angry man. But when you say that a woman *should* be kind, and particularly when you say she should be kind to the man in her life, it somehow takes on a different meaning. In

Cooking as Nurturing

For years, I was a candidate for Microwavers Anonymous, if there were such a thing. To me, cooking was lame. I had apartment after apartment where the stove would go virtually untouched and the refrigerator didn't hold as much as a quart of milk. My specialty was curbside pickup takeout. And the idea of having to cook for a man? Ludicrous and insulting. I told all my boyfriends that I was committed to a lifetime of making enough money to eat at restaurants three meals a day.

Then one day a very wise woman in my life—a mother of five, happily married twenty years—said something very simple to me: "Nurturing is a good thing, Tracy. And cooking is a big part of nurturing." It had never occurred to me that cooking for myself and others was really a form of caring for the people I loved, including myself—one I was terrible at. And what I couldn't do for myself, I certainly couldn't do for a man, either.

So I started cooking. First, easy stuff like roasted beets, or chicken in a Crock-Pot. Then I expanded to include some pastas and soups. Soon I was whipping up all kinds of yumminess. (Ask me about my pork loin!) Now, when a new man comes into my life, I am sure to cook for him in the first few dates. It's *fun*, and you wouldn't believe how much they appreciate it.

What I've learned is that for a man, if you're willing to cook *and* be nice, it's like winning both showcases in the Showcase Showdown. Because food is more than sustenance. It is love. After all, you'd be willing to cook for your children, wouldn't you? So then why would you withhold it from your man?

women, the idea that kindness is a very, very important thing to be comes across to many people as oppressive. As if a woman has to disown or repress a part of herself to practice kindness, especially to her man.

I would just like to say *this is bullshit.*

So how do you change a behavior you would change if you could, but you can't, so you don't?

Spiritual Stuff That Will Help You Change

You're going to need to do some spiritual stuff. Like I said, this whole book is based on the idea that marriage is a spiritual path. Maybe it doesn't have to be a spiritual path for everyone—perhaps Donald Trump doesn't give a crap about all this stuff—but maybe it does for you if you want to be married but it just doesn't seem to be happening.

In general, spiritual stuff is things you don't want to do, or stuff that you think is only done by people like Mother Teresa or Angelina Jolie. Your mind will tell you it is a waste of time, or you've already tried it, or it's too hard. But you have to tell your mind to take a time-out. Because *doing spiritual stuff works.* It works better than vodka, Pilates, or shopping. But—and here's the catch—it doesn't feel good until after you've already done it.

We'll talk more about spiritual stuff as we go along, but let's start with first things first. What's the spiritual solution for bitch energy?

Forgiveness. If you can truly forgive, your anger will evaporate. And with it will go the driving force behind the bitchiness. Forgiveness is letting yourself, your mom, your old boyfriend, and everyone else who ever hurt you—even if they hurt you really badly—off the hook. Not because you're the bigger person, but because you finally get that *there is no hook.* What we call the hook is really just the condition of being human—which means being deeply flawed in ways that *will,* sooner or later, hurt another person. Who among us hasn't fucked another person up? I'll tell you who: nobody! Sure, some of us are doing better than others, but it's kind of arrogant to get all *proud* about it—after all, as long as I'm alive, I've got another chance to fall short. To be human.

The key to walking through life without retreating into your bitch—and becoming angry, fearful, and defensive—is to forgive. So how do you do that? The best way is to *change your story.* Change the way you think and talk about what has gone down in your life—especially the things that have disappointed you or made you angry. Story is one of the most powerful tools you have. It's how you—and all people—shape their experience. That's why those prehistoric folks in France made those little cave drawings. They wanted to make sure that everyone for the next thirty-two thousand years knew about all the buffalo they were hunting down and killing. They defined themselves by it.

We tell ourselves, and other people, stories about who we are, what happened to us, and what the world is like. We bring our story with us on every date and into every relationship we have. What few people realize is that the stories you tell about yourself essentially become true—because the story shapes your thinking, the thinking shapes your perception, the perception shapes your choices, the choices shape your actions, and your actions are ultimately your destiny.

Did you get that? This story thing is *huge.*

The cool thing is that you have absolute unilateral power over your own story. Sure, other people will try (and they will try *hard*) to get you to accept *their* version of your story, but they don't actu-

Snip the Elastic

One way to think of forgiveness is to picture trying on a pair of shoes at Target—you know, the ones that have those elastic thingies to ensure that both shoes stay together. Whoever or whatever you're mad at, you're tied to that thing. Not only that, but you're also tied to whatever you believe they did to you. You think what they did is *who you are.*

And you know how when you try on those Target shoes and forget that they're tied together and you take an actual person-sized step? You almost fall over because the elastic thing is only two inches long. That's exactly how anger, fear, and defensiveness limit your forward motion. They trip you up—and also make you look really foolish, right there in the middle of the shoe department at Target.

Forgiveness is choosing to snip the elastic that is holding you in one place. And the only person who can snip the elastic is *you.* You have to make a decision that you no longer want to be bound to the past. For a while, you might notice that you're still taking tiny steps, as if your shoes are still tethered together. But little by little, as you practice forgiveness, you will find yourself feeling more open, more loving, more free.

ally have the power to make you do so. It is imperative that you shape your story in ways that empower you, not piss you off or turn you into the victim.

I'll share with you the best example of this in my own life. As I said, I was a foster child. Until I started shaping my own story for myself, here is a basic sketch of what I was working with: I was born. My mom, Linda, gave me up. My dad, Freddie, went to jail. And I went into a series of foster homes, finally landing in a good one, where I stayed for four years. Then my dad got out of prison and came back to claim me, taking me to live with his girlfriend. He ended up going back to prison shortly after that, and I stayed with the girlfriend, who was no picnic, until I was eighteen. There's more, but you get the idea.

In short, my understanding of my life was the super-dramatic after-school-special version of the story: *Tracy M.: Unwanted, Unloved, and Alone.* Obviously, if I insist on seeing myself as a victim, there's a lot to work with here. I have plenty to be pissed about as far as Linda and Freddie are concerned. They were some terrible parents. And I got shafted. Right?

Wrong. Because that is only one way to assemble the facts.

Here's the spiritual-stuff version of the story: I got born. After a mere twelve Saturday nights, I took a look around at my pimping, criminal dad and prostitute, alcoholic mom and said to myself, "Surely I can do better than this." I got my ass out of there and (after some unfortunate pit stops that taught me a lot about life and people) somehow managed to secure myself a very nice spot with a Lutheran minister and his wife and their five kids, where I got to experience a middle-class existence, go to a great private school, and have the kind of safe, stable life I *never* would have had with Linda and Freddie. Then, well before I would have come into some ridiculously huge adolescent conflict with those wonderful but super-conservative people, I ended up in the home of a feminist, first-generation hipster who exposed me to lots of radical ideas, made sure I went to good schools, taught me about art, and, perhaps most important, let me watch endless hours of television—thus setting the stage for my current career as a television writer.

Guess which version of this movie has the happy ending?

I want you to start thinking about how you can flip the script on your life. Especially the places you have the most pain: that bad post-college breakup, the long lonely streak since you turned thirty, the stupid childhood, the major career disappointment. See if you can shift the story, just a little, toward something that doesn't make you feel quite so bad. And if you can make yourself laugh, all the better.

Creating a new belief system is a little like blocking a freeway exit, permanently. When you find yourself tooling down the freeway trying to get off again at your old story—how your parents screwed you over, or how men are jackasses, or how there's something wrong with you—you need to sail past that exit and instead take the off-ramp for your new story. At first it's really annoying and you keep forgetting that your usual exit is closed. You will often have to backtrack, go around things, or detour miles out of your way. You will feel like you're running very late. But eventually you figure out a new exit. You no longer unconsciously keep taking the old one, and you happily discover something amazing: you have arrived somewhere other than Compton.

What Your Best Friend Knows but Hasn't Told You

So let's summarize what we've covered in Chapter 1 by taking a cold hard look at what no one has been willing to say straight to your face:

- **You're a bitch.** You're not nice, and guys don't want to marry you because of it. Not because they're misogynists, but because no one wants to spend their life with someone who is angry all the time.
- **Bitchiness is really anger and defensiveness.** The anger looks justified, which is why it seems so righteous. But who cares? To paraphrase an old saying, would you rather be right or be married?
- **Be nice.** This is so basic, you should know it already. But for some reason you're thinking you can be critical and judgmental of men and they will want to be with you for a lifetime anyway. They won't.
- **Learn to forgive.** Being nice won't happen until you learn to forgive. You have to let people—especially men—off the hook, because there isn't one. Forgiving people also makes you smile more and look even prettier.
- **Get a new story.** This is the best way to forgive. Be creative! It's your life, and you only live once. Change your narrative to empower yourself and the underground anger that is the driving force behind bitchiness will naturally disappear.

2. You're Shallow

Or, Getting What You Want, and Other Lies

1. Are you holding out for a guy of a certain height or income level?
2. Do friends say you're too picky, but you just feel like you have high standards?
3. Have you passed on a good guy because he doesn't look/dress/earn the way you wanted?

IMAGINE A GUY WHO ONLY WANTS TO DATE BLONDES. Preferably with a C-cup or bigger. He goes to parties, chats with some perfectly nice women—women like you, maybe—but he doesn't want to know about anyone with ten extra pounds or cankles. When friends suggest he loosen his standards just a bit—maybe try a brunette, or go out on a few dates with a 7.1 just to see if a spark might happen, he says he's sorry, but it all comes down to chemistry and he only feels it for 8s, 9s, and 10s.

What do you think of this guy? You think he's a douche, right?

But if you're a woman who wants a man of a certain height, or with a wallet of a certain thickness, or with a particular kind of job, education, or family background, you are not really any different from the man who wants a woman with big boobs or blond hair. That guy you have no respect for, the one you think—no, you *know*—is lame? Well, that guy is *you*.

I hate to say this, but . . . *you're shallow.*

Shallow is when you are more concerned with how a man looks than how he *is*. It's when you care more about what your friends will think of him than how you feel about him when you're alone together. It's when you can't stop wishing that if he dressed a little better, looked a little cuter, had a slightly more interesting job, or possessed way more money, you might be willing to consider him for real.

Being shallow is not okay. Not just because it's not very nice (see Chapter 1, "You're a Bitch") but also because when a good man encounters a shallow woman, his heart freezes over. Which means he might be willing to fool around with you for a little while, but he's never going to sign a mortgage with you.

What It's Really About

Being shallow is about perfectionism. You won't settle for something that's good enough—it has got to be *ideal*. You want every single need and desire you have to be satisfied, preferably right now, by finding, dating, and marrying the one person who *has it all*. Never mind that no one has it all—certainly not you!

The problem with perfectionism is that it is so dehumanizing. It causes you to see people not as human beings but as things. Objects. Have you ever heard the saying "The perfect is the enemy of the good"? That's what happens when you allow yourself to give in to your perfectionist tendencies.

Perfectionism causes you to objectify men. You've probably heard this term before, maybe in a women's studies class or from a feminist person—just not applied to yourself. Here's a definition from Wikipedia: "Objectification is an attitude that regards a person as a commodity or as an object for use."

This is a very fancy way of saying *you're using someone,* the way you would use, say, a can opener, or the remote control for the TV. To objectify someone is to treat them as a tool, a means to an end. You decide what role he is going to fill in your life, then your perfectionism makes you decide which qualities—physical, professional, emotional, intellectual—you "need" him to have in order to fulfill that role. Then you set out with your checklist to find the guy who has it all.

What most people are looking for (unconsciously, of course) in a partner is someone who is going to reflect back their favorite aspects of themselves, make their life better than it is now, and allow them to stay comfortable—in other words, someone who is going to be just like a blow-up doll, except with more interesting sex. Because real human beings do not just do what you tell them to and reflect back your best self. Except, perhaps, on your wedding day.

Eventually, everyone discovers that, no matter how much you have in common, your partner is not now, and never will be, you. Add to that the probability that your partner came into marriage hoping *you* were gonna be doing some reflecting back at *him* and that *you* were going to make *his* life better, and it gets obvious real quick that no one around here is going to be allowed to stay comfortable. More likely, attempts to stay comfortable will cause horrible *dis*comfort. But then, that's what objectifying another person gets you. What else would you expect from rubbing up against a love object made out of latex?

Everyone knows women get objectified—you've seen *Playboy,* right?—but men get objectified, too. Not necessarily for their six-pack abs or shiny hair, though sometimes for that reason. No, we objectify men for other things: the resources they can provide for us (money, a nice home, a decent car to drive), their ability to protect us, and maybe most of all their sperm, which will become our babies. (And boy, do we want our babies!)

So how do you know when you're objectifying someone? Here's one way: you tend to pay attention only to men who have what you quote-unquote "want."

Let's say a friend invites you to a dinner party. You ask who is going to be there. She names a few people, some couples and a handful of men, none of whom you're familiar with. You ask who they are, what they do. You even look up a couple of them right then and there on Google or Facebook. What you discover is not all that interesting. You find your willingness to attend the party beginning to droop. You beg off, saying you're not sure but maybe you have a conflicting engagement that night—and by conflicting engagement, you mean the four episodes of *Private Practice* taking up valuable space on your TiVo.

If it never occurs to you to put your own agenda aside for one night and maybe boost your friend's dinner party by actually *being* a great guest, if you regularly decide that you're not interested in talking to men *without even meeting them,* if you find yourself on dates rejecting guys after they say one or two things you just know you can't deal with . . . I can assure you, you're shallow.

Objectifying someone causes you to focus on the things about a person that aren't important and overlook the things that are. Like, for instance, character. It also makes people feel awful. A tall, good-looking, rich guy who is smart wants to know that a woman loves him for who he is, not for his bank account, face, or body. I think this is why you sometimes see a man who has the kind of resources that would allow him to have his pick of women yet has chosen to be with a woman who is maybe not that spectacular-looking. I always imagine that she's a fantastic person who gave him the gift of seeing him beyond what he had to offer materially.

Notes from My Life as a Teen Wife

When I was nineteen, I moved to San Francisco with my soon-to-be first husband. With not a lot of skills (unless you count smoking cigarettes a skill), I took a job as one of those girls who spray perfume on you at Macy's. I worked mostly at Union Square, the center of the San Francisco retail universe and the point through which every tourist there eventually passes. For a girl from Minneapolis, it was beyond exciting. I felt like I was living the dream.

But I'm the ambitious type, so I wasn't content to just choke some people in a cloud of Giorgio. In minutes I had worked my way up to the next level of success in the cosmetics world: the girl who puts makeup on you at Macy's. Here's what I learned doing the makeup of regular ladies passing through Union Square: *everyone is beautiful.*

I'm not kidding. I'd be standing there at the counter with some nice mom of two from Walnut Creek, California, or Charlotte, North Carolina, perched in my tall chair. She might be feeling a little weird that she was letting me—a girl who still littered her speech with the big "oh, *reel*ly" of the Minnesota home I'd only just left—wield sable brushes two inches in front of her face. Somewhere between the foundation and the mascara, I would invariably notice something special on her, like the most exquisitely curved brow. Or maybe a business lady who dashed up to the counter on her lunch hour would have super-gorgeous skin, or complex green eyes flecked with bright brown and ringed with navy blue. Stuff like that.

Often the things I saw weren't the kind of thing you'd notice on a first date. I had to get right up in these women's faces, and perhaps more important, I had to be objective about them. I wasn't putting eyeliner on them thinking about taking an up-or-down vote on whether I wanted to sleep with them, marry them, and have their children, or even whether I ever wanted to see them again. I had to be open-minded to see what they had to offer, and I had to look closely.

I once had a boyfriend who was, how shall I say, *interesting*-looking. He was what the French would call, in women, *jolie laide*, literally "pretty-ugly"—attractive but not conventionally good-looking. His chin was a bit weak, his nose was a bit strong, his eyes were a bit . . . asymmetrical. When we first started dating, there were times when I would look at his face and think, "Wait, what?"

At first I even thought about breaking it off. Not only was his style completely different from mine—much more conservative—but everything about him physically was not what I was used to. But I stuck with it, in part because he had—seriously—a sparkling personality. He really did. He was one of the funniest, most mild-mannered, most agreeable people I have ever met.

We stayed together for a good amount of time, and somewhere along the line my eye . . . adjusted. He had a ton of beauty; I just had to look at him differently to see it. It's like tuning in a radio station on an old-school car radio, where if you dial infinitesimally to the right, you can catch the amazing radio station from two towns over that plays the best oldies or whatever. I could see this other thing in him—how bright his eyes were, the amazing color of his skin when he'd been out playing (too much, way too much) soccer, his physical coordination and grace. Ultimately, loving that not-so-perfect-looking man made me aware of a whole other level of beauty that, even though we're no longer together, I can still access and appreciate.

Years later, I learned this same lesson the opposite way, from a truly gorgeous boyfriend I had named Brandon. He was beautiful, with thick dark curly hair, enormous blue eyes, and facial symmetry that made you want to find the nearest hotel room. Brandon looked like Snow White if she were a really, really hot guy. We stayed together three years, and during that time I discovered that (unfortunately) the effect of beauty is often like any other effect: eventually it wears off. Usually sooner. It's not that Brandon ceased to be gorgeous—the hordes of other women sniffing around all the time were proof of that. It's that his beauty *ceased to change the way I felt about him.* It didn't make me willing to put up with his bullshit (and he had a ton of bullshit; after all, he was in his early twenties), and it certainly didn't make him grow up any faster.

I guess what I'm saying is, beauty is in the eye of the beholder. And the choice of what to behold is yours. Of course you have to have a baseline physical attraction to someone (which we'll talk more about a little later), but given that, you're going to want to choose wisely. Because no one, not even you, is going to be young and good-looking forever.

Why Natalie's Not Married

Not all perfectionism is about looks. Check out my friend Natalie. Nat's a good-looking girl—big brown eyes, and *such* a cute figure—who loves her job as a wardrobe stylist on movies and television shows. But when it comes to dating, Natalie acts like a worker at a fruit-processing plant. I can just see her standing next to the conveyor belt, carefully scrutinizing what's on offer, then

plucking out all the man-apples with blemishes, dots, bird peckings, and bruises and tossing them aside. Natalie only wants the
apples like the ones at the big chain supermarket: flawless. Great
job, great body, great personality, and great family.

What I keep trying to tell Natalie is that even if she does manage to locate one of these seemingly perfect man-apples and get
into a relationship with him, she will quickly discover that there
were some blemishes, bird peckings, and bruises she missed on
the conveyor belt. (There always are.) Then she will have to grap-
ple with the tendency to focus on those flaws *inside* the
relationship—a battle she will lose, because she's a perfectionist.
Then there is the truest thing of all: *perfect-looking produce doesn't
taste like anything!*

What Natalie thinks she has is standards. What I think Natalie
has is a case of the unrealistic pickies. Natalie is so choosy about
what she wants in a man—he should have a really good job and a
great education; he has to be a homeowner; he should dress well,
be familiar with the latest stars of the art world, and enjoy Fellini
films and Thai food; and if at all possible, he should be a vegetar-
ian and drive a hybrid, do yoga, and preferably have some kind of
spiritual practice—she will *never* find a guy who has it all. At
some level she must know this, since she's thirty-eight and in
twenty-five years of dating still hasn't found someone who meets
all her criteria. It's just not realistic.

What Natalie should do is pick two (possibly three) deal break-
ers from her list—the things she absolutely *must have*—and let
the rest go. Because when you're faced with an actual human
being, sometimes things that you'd think you just couldn't deal
with suddenly turn out to be not that big a deal. The other factor
is that being in a relationship matures a person, so what Natalie
considers a deal breaker now might just be a preference five years

down the road. But Natalie doesn't know that, because in many ways she's still very immature.

Some Relevant Stuff About Men

A friend of mine told me a story about her teenage son that illustrates the point perfectly. On the first day of high school, she noticed he wasn't wearing the blue and white striped T-shirt she had carefully laid out for him. Instead, he'd chosen to wear a different, more fashion-forward T-shirt. When she asked about it, the teen said the striped shirt just wasn't the "right kind." Apparently the days of not caring what other people thought were officially over. (At least until adolescence passes—which, from the looks of the dating pool, might be around age forty-two.)

I tell you this story in a chapter on shallowness because in order to make a good marriage, you are going to have to get rid of everything on your list that is coming from the part of you that wants to wear the right shirt for the first day of high school because of what other people might think. If you're still pursuing a long (or even long*ish*) list of shallow wants, chances are you are still thinking like a teenager. Unless you are planning to be someone's trophy wife, adolescent thinking will tend to keep you from getting married. And even if you do manage to wangle a husband who fits your list, the marriage itself will be sort of shallow. How could it be anything else? It's all based on superficialities.

A key feature of adulthood is letting go of what other people think and making choices that are *right for you* even if other people don't approve of or understand them. In adolescence, you're looking around, checking to make sure you're wearing the "right" shoes and the "right" shirt. Which is perfectly appropriate— when you're sixteen.

But if you are still making life decisions based on what your peers will think of your choice, you are going to miss your own boat! Adulthood is about committing to the person you know yourself to be—or at least the person you suspect that you are. (Or will be, when you get your shit together.) By the time you are a grown-up, you know that perfection doesn't exist. Which means you are going to have to take a different approach to the men you're choosing.

Which brings me to the sensitive topic of the way you present yourself.

Growing up in Minnesota, we used to go fishing. We'd take out a boat and drop the anchor, and we'd have tackle boxes with all sorts of lures and whatnot. There were all sorts of fish down there. But not every fish would go for every type of bait. Some only went for worms. Others liked those shiny spinners. Still others preferred minnows. You'd bait your hook based on what you wanted to catch.

This is true of mating, too. You've got to figure out what you're fishing for. This means you want to make sure you're mindful of the way you will be perceived. That's my subtle way of saying don't dress or act like a slut!

If you are looking to form a long-term partnership, you probably don't want to overly promote your sexual assets. I said *overly* promote. Go ahead, look cute! Show your figure! Put on another coat of mascara! Those are all fine things. But if your presentation—and really, I'm talking less about your cleavage than about your *vibe*—promises more sex partner than life partner, it is not going to help you attract a long-term mate. While most guys want a sexually attractive partner, they don't want to spend the next forty years fighting off all the men who are going to come nosing around because you just love a pair of Lucite heels.

Face vs. Body

Evolutionary psychologists at the University of Texas recently published some really interesting findings that may have you reconsidering all those hours spent in the gym. They found that men interested in short-term companionship (like a one-night stand) showed more interest in a woman's body, while men looking for a long-term relationship were more interested in a woman's face.

The researchers asked 375 college students to look at a picture of a potential mate. At the beginning of the experiment both face and body were hidden. Researchers then gave them the option of looking at the face or the body, but not both. The results were fascinating. Only one-quarter of the men who were evaluating the image as a potential long-term mate chose to look at the body. But for a short-term mate? Fifty-one percent of men chose to see the body.

Researchers theorized that the body showed clues to a woman's fertility—important if you're planning to "hit it and quit it." On the other hand, the face showed clues to a woman's character—something only a man interested in a long-term relationship would care about.

Perhaps not surprisingly, women showed *no significant difference* between faces or bodies when looking for short-term or long-term mates. We'll enjoy sex with a cad just as much as sex with a guy who loves us.

How You're Going to Have to Change

Start by giving up on the idea of *getting what you want*. Don't panic. As it turns out, you don't actually need what you want. What you really want is what you *need*. See, as far as I'm concerned, the Rolling Stones were wrong: you *can* (very often) get what you want. I've seen a million chicks go out there and get what they wanted. Happens every day. If only that were the problem! There's actually a much bigger issue: not only do you probably not *really* know what you want, but even if you did know, once you got it, you wouldn't want it anymore, because . . .

No one in the history of humankind ever became happy by getting what they wanted.

Just ask anyone who's ever won the lottery, an Academy Award, or the final rose on *The Bachelor*. Oh, sure, they're happy—for about twenty minutes. Then that old restless pang returns, and soon they're itching to win *another* lottery, *another* Oscar, *another* bachelor, or at the very least have sex with a stranger and go on a major shopping spree at Barneys.

There is just something in the human condition that makes it impossible to be happy forevermore from getting something. Anything. Even the perfect husband. So just forget it. There's no need to make long lists of what you want, and no need to page through thousands of pictures online looking for someone cute enough. Your new want is to find a guy who is *what you need.*

So let's talk about what you need and how you go about getting it. The usual understanding of this is that a chick stands there and unscrolls a long list of "needs"—this, that, and the other thing— that is just a list of "wants" by another name. I mean something different. When I use the phrase "what you need," I mean a man who has the qualities that are going to help you grow to your high-

Intention Box

When I talk about setting intentions, what I mean is making a formal declaration about something—even if you're only declaring it to yourself. Sometimes it helps to actually create a little ritual around declaring something; it makes it feel more real.

One way to do this is to create an Intention Box. All you need is a small box, like a jewelry box, or maybe one of those little decorated boxes you find at an imports or vintage store. Then take a small piece of paper and write down your intention. It can be about some way you imagine your life looking (*I'm in a beautiful sunny home, surrounded by children*) or perhaps a problem you're trying to find a solution to. Go ahead and use a beautiful piece of paper and colored pens if it makes the ritual more fun for you, but it doesn't really matter. You can even draw pictures—it's up to you. All you really want to do is to get your declaration down in a way that makes it *feel* like you mean it. Then put it in the box and leave it there. When you close the box, try to know that whatever it is you just put in there *is already done*.

Every time you pass the box or notice it, remind yourself that everything in there *is already done*—already taken care of, or being taken care of. This is a really powerful way to start picturing your life. Every time you think of another declaration, write it down and put it in the box. After a year, open the box and read your declarations. I bet a lot of them are already in your life.

est expression as a human being. In return, you have qualities that are going to help him grow to *his* highest expression.

The thing is, you have to assume that, quite possibly (even probably), you have *no idea* what these qualities are. So you don't need to list them, because you couldn't if you tried. Possibly your closest friends could get together and come up with something relevant, but that won't really be necessary. Nor will you need (necessarily) to spend forty-five minutes answering a question-naire online, or become an amateur copywriter by filling out the most compelling profile ever posted on PlentyOfFish.com. There's a much easier way to discover what you need.

Here's how. First you set the intention to be with a man whom you can help grow to his highest expression (and who can help you grow to yours), then you *see who shows up.* If you have set the intention to be with such a man and actively maintain that inten-tion, whoever blows into your life—even if it's just for a week or a month—will present you with an opportunity to expand yourself (and vice versa) in precisely the ways you need to expand.

How can I be so sure? Because I know that what you need at any given moment in time is usually right on top of the pile. This is how life works. Metaphorically speaking, while you're looking for that particular T-shirt you just *have* to wear tonight, life has calmly placed the perfect top to go with those jeans right where you can see it, and even better—it's clean! All you have to do is put it on.

For whatever reason, this area of a relationship—getting what you want versus trusting that life will give you what you need—is where many women are highly resistant to change. Like my friend Kim. A gorgeous woman with an amazing head of curls, Kim is pretty sure about what she needs: the type of guy found hanging around a yacht club. Possibly because Kim, twenty-seven, has the

Notice What You Don't Have

Think of all the things you've wanted in your life that you didn't get: the lead in the eighth-grade school play. The Sergeant Pepper jacket from the Balmain 2009 collection. That guy named Owen with the curly hair from Pittsburgh. The six-figure job straight out of college.

Now ask yourself how many of those things you still want. And are you okay not having gotten them?

In a way, this is the companion exercise to the Intention Box. It teaches you not to get too specific about what you think your life needs to look like, because when you really examine your past wants, it becomes clear that you didn't need all of them. Many of the whatevers and whomevers you think you want right now are going to end up in that same time capsule, a cute footnote to your history. So you might as well build that into your understanding of the situation right now, instead of wasting a bunch of time on a fantasy of some particular life you're going to have with a particular guy.

shapeliest, most *Dancing with the Stars*–worthy legs imaginable, she will not settle for anything less than a total catch. She wants a high-earning, tall, broad-shouldered, full-head-of-hair hunk. She doesn't say this out loud, but she works hard to look good, she has a high-profile job in PR, and I know she feels, at some level, *deserving* of a guy who will drop as many jaws as she does.

Kim goes out on dates pretty much every weekend—lots of them, because she's very good-looking—and when we talk afterward she'll often admit that she probably *should* have been interested. The bottom line is that Kim can't get excited about a man she considers a "dweeb." But what Kim calls a dweeb, I call marriage material. After all what has dating all those Total Catches done for her so far besides keep her single when she no longer wants to be?

Let's focus a minute on what the shallow girl "wants" anyway. I'd say 98 percent of them have one of two wants: *hot guys* and *rich guys*. They want someone who is going to fulfill the fantasy of perfect sex and attraction (with beautiful babies, of course) and/or make enough money so they can live in a pretty house in a choice neighborhood *without* having to work at a semi-meaningless job. In some ways, shallow girls aren't shallow so much as they are hopeful. They dream of a certain life with a certain kind of man, and they don't want to give up that dream. The problem is that when they hold out for so long, they end up sailing right past their mid-thirties. And really, what exactly is it that they're waiting for? Let's break it down, starting with hot guys.

The shallow girl is often ruled by her need for *chemistry*. There is a notion that what a person is attracted to is ironclad. It's not really that simple. The way I see it, there are roughly three types of attraction:

1. ***Oh, hell no!*** You are absolutely flat in his presence, or even totally repulsed. You're pretty sure your genes just aren't a match, and this is how nature is keeping you away from him. It is Just. Not. Happening. Okay, fine, you don't have to date this guy, but don't be mean to him, either.

2. ***Oh, hell YES!*** This is the guy where the sexual attraction is so intense, you want to marry him from his picture on the Internet. The key to dating from this chemical starting point is to know *which kind of guy attracts you like this*. If in the past you were

insanely attracted like this to two or three guys (one isn't a big enough sample) who turned out to have a job at IBM and want a serious commitment of marriage and children, then by all means *go for it*! But if the guys *you* feel this kind of attraction for are more the commitment-phobe, bad boy, liar, cheater, sociopath, etc.—stay away. Why choose pain? You will do yourself a tremendous favor if you just decide in advance that it won't be different this time.

3. *Hmmm, I wonder . . .* This is the guy you end up talking to for an hour at the party even though you didn't really even notice him come in. You're a little surprised to find yourself enjoying the conversation and at one point you even look at him and wonder if you could ever kiss him and if you did, what it would be like. You are not sure. You can't really even *see* how that would happen, necessarily, yet you find yourself sitting there considering it. *Hmmm, I wonder . . .*

I want you to start dating a lot of number threes. Just know that you won't really figure out what's in store for you with this guy until you've at the very least kissed him, and more likely not until you've been in a relationship with him for, say, ninety days. The type of relationship based on this sort of attraction has an *unfolding* quality—it's more complex, which is part of the reason it has a tendency to lead to commitment. The bottom line: go for a guy you're *interested* in, not necessarily super hot for.

The catch-22 about chemistry—as most of us have figured out by now—is that we seem to have the most of it with the *least appropriate men.* For me it's possibly because my mom and dad were all kinds of a mess—but your parents don't have to be as bad as mine. Maybe your dad was just the kind of guy who liked to flirt or drink or gamble, and your mom had rage issues or was really

He's Foxy, and He's Just Your Type

A girlfriend was recently telling me about a guy she had her eye on. She's thirty-two and dearly wants to settle down and have a marriage and a baby. But here she is on the phone, enthusing that the guy she's into is "foxy." As if that's a good thing.

Girlfriend: Seriously, Trace. He's so foxy.
Me: Foxy? What in the world do you want with foxy? Foxes go into henhouses and kill chickens.

Foxy isn't just good-looking. Foxy is a state of mind. In the animal world, foxes hunt girl chicks and steal their eggs. That's what they do in the dating world, too. In my experience, foxiness is inversely related to commitment. At this point in my life—in fact, at any point in my life past the age of, oh, about twenty-three—I would rather not subject myself to a foxy man, in much the same way I no longer eat a whole big bag of M&M's. It's going to be amazing while I'm doing it, but I have absolutely no doubt that at some point afterward I'm going to feel bad enough to wonder whether it was actually worth it. And since I know only two women who actually married their foxy guys (and one of them has a Pilates reformer installed *in her house*), chances are very good that Mr. Foxy won't last long enough to make it worth the trouble.

controlling or a hypochondriac—that would be enough to get you some pretty great chemistry with some pretty lame guys. In fact, you can tell how you experienced your parents energetically (and especially where they hurt you) by what you keep finding yourself dealing with in relationships.

My thing used to be going for the slick womanizer. Like this dude I used to crush on, Justin. Super good-looking, with a major Hollywood career—this guy has what women want and he knows it. One time, while sandwiched into a tiny, packed art gallery, Justin sidled past me. And just as he brushed past (his front to my back, *swoon*) he dropped his hand to mine and brushed his fingers on the inside of my palm. *The inside of my palm!* Talk about chemistry—I knew if I allowed myself to go there, glass beakers were going to be shattering big-time.

However, as tempting as it might have been, I'd already learned from my third husband where that kind of man takes you—and it was an experience I didn't need to have again. I knew to stop right there. Freeze. Start doing some critical thinking. Exactly who was this Justin character I had the "amazing" chemistry with? Let's take a closer look:

- He's never been in a long-term relationship.
- He's just about to turn forty but tends to date women (girls, really) in their twenties, because he can. The women you see on his arm tend to look like Audrina from *The Hills* if she had gone to college, or maybe was Asian.
- The guy's Facebook profile pic used to show him in a bathrobe, drinking martinis.
- He drives a vintage muscle car.

That's only four things, and it's already obvious that Justin may be a stone fox, but *he is not going to be anyone's husband in the next few minutes.* At least not anyone's *good* husband. Sure, maybe when he's forty-seven he'll scoop up a twenty-eight-year-old knockout and give her a baby or two. But you know that by the time those kids are five and seven, he is going to be brushing the palm of that hot mom at the big school fund-raising event. *Yikes.* And thank God, I don't have to be his wife pretending not to notice.

Okay, so you've got it that hot guys are not all they're cracked up to be. Now let's talk about rich guys. The guys with the kick-ass job, apartment, car, and/or bank account. Obviously, partnering with someone who knows how to hold a job and is successful at paying his rent each month (however much or little that is) is a good thing.

But you know you're wading around in the shallow end of the dating pool when you actually *pass* on a decent guy with a stable job, someone you might go, "Hmmm, I wonder . . ." about, in order to *wait* for a high earner you're convinced you're wildly attracted to.

What few shallow chicks think about is that while there are definite advantages to marrying a man with a large income, there are also disadvantages—which no one ever talks about. But after fourteen years as a mom in and around the entertainment business, I've made a few observations about the differences between middle-class dads and rich-guy dads.

1. *Rich guys are never home.* Okay, not never. But they are certainly home way less than the men who make the middle-class money. No one pays you umpteen figures because you go in at 9:00 a.m. and leave at 5:00 p.m.

2. *The marriages of high-earning men tend to be very traditional.* Someone has to be at home taking care of the kids and things, and when there's a lot of money and the wife doesn't work, that someone tends to be her. From what I've seen, this arrangement works best when the kids are really small—under age four. Because as the kids grow older whatever career you used to have sort of fades into the background, and by the time ten years have passed, there's a pretty serious inequity going on. No one wants to say this out loud, because usually these ladies have very nice houses, children, and lives. If you prefer a more traditional thing, this could work out well for you. You just have to know what kind of woman you are and make sure you don't sell yourself out for a dream that isn't really even yours.

3. *The wives of rich men* do *have a job—house manager.* Running a household is a lot of work, especially when it's a big, nice house. And when you have a husband who makes a lot of money, he is generally not thinking that he's going to be splitting the laundry with you fifty-fifty. Nor will he be packing lunches (no one told you private schools often don't have a cafeteria!), doing the carpool, or waiting for the plumber to arrive. All of that's *your* job when you have a half-a-million-dollar-a-year man. You might figure you'll have the money to hire someone to do all that for you, but even if you have round-the-clock maids, it will be your job to hire them, manage them, fire them, and, of course, do their job when they're sick. Which means not only do you miss out on having a partner to help you with all that work, but your kids miss out on watching a man do all that as well. And did we really fight for all that equality in the 1970s and '80s just to go back to the '50s? Maybe.

4. *Rich guys can make it hard to remarry.* Divorce almost always sucks, but when you were married to a rich guy, it can be even worse. You might have things paid for, but chances are you will be on your own far more than the ex-wife of the man who makes regular-guy money, owing to the abovementioned Rich Guy Issue #1. The other thing is that if you do divorce, it can be harder to find another mate. Few dudes feel comfortable dating or marrying a woman who is basically being taken care of by another man. The ex has too much power over her.

Finding a wealthy guy could potentially present you with almost as many problems as it solves. So how do you move from checking your list twice to dating someone super nice?

Spiritual Stuff That Will Help You Change

This is where a lot of girls will say to me—in a really intense voice—"Are you saying I *can't* go out with guys I'm attracted to?"

Calm down, ladies. I'm not saying you have to *give up* on finding someone you like. What I'm asking you to do is delve deeper into the idea of what you're attracted to, and question your assumptions about it. Attraction is not necessarily something that just "happens" to you. It's a dynamic process that gives you lots of room to make all sorts of choices—some of which will work better for you than others.

Another thing about chemistry: I know it's about pheromones or whatever, but on a spiritual level, I think it's about something else. I believe the thing that draws two particular people together—right after lust, height, money, his blue eyes, or whatever else it is you *think* you like him for—is that there is something these two people have to learn from each other that no one else can help them learn. And by help, I mean give them so much grief that there is no way in hell the other person has any chance of escaping the lesson.

Not that they can't try. That's called divorce and people do it every day. But as I can well tell you, in no way does it mean that you've evaded your life lesson. It just means you'll be doing it with some other partner, who can point to your rotten track record and conclude that whatever's going on in your relationship with him is probably your fault. And you will have very little in the way of a defense, because you've been down that road before. So if the guy you already have is decent, you might as well stick it out.

And this is where another big spiritual idea storms onto the stage: that what you are is what you get. Sometimes this is called the law of attraction. It can mean a lot of things, but in this case it means that your match will always be, well, your match. So if what you are is shallow, then that's what you'll attract. No exceptions. Like always attracts like. The Zen Buddhist says it like this: *As above, so below.* Or *As within, so without.*

As an example, let's go back to the beginning of this chapter, to the guy who only wants to date the 8s, 9s, and 10s. Derek's a doctor, six feet tall, attractive, with a great 401k and a very promising future. Derek thinks most women are out for money. (Not all women, actually. Just the really attractive ones.) He doesn't even *realize* how committed he is to this idea—which makes him a perfect match for the women who don't know they're objectifying men.

But if you listen closely, you can tell. Give him a couple drinks (okay, four) and get him talking about women. Derek's a guy who will say out loud that chicks only like him because he's a physician (how come doctors never want to call themselves doctors?) and because when they see him roll up (in his Range Rover, mind you) they break out in dollar signs. Clearly, not every woman is like this, but interestingly, about 95 percent of the women who *meet with Derek's approval* are.

What's even more interesting to me is that few of Derek's girl-friends actually started life as an 8. Just as Derek went looking for a bigger number, so did the women with whom he found himself in relationships. They added a few tenths to their score in the usual ways: pumping up the hair color a few shades, going from walking workouts to hard-core spinning four or five times a week, and in the case of at least two of them, springing for the bigger breasts or the smaller nose.

There's nothing wrong with these things, but neither is it coincidental that these "improvements" are what made them attractive to a guy like Derek. When people—whether male or female—approach themselves as objects in order to "catch" the other objects, they only end up with the opposite-sex version of themselves. Sometimes this works—he makes money, she spends her days looking cute—but there's way more fun to be had inside a good marriage than that. And though Derek is clearly choosing these women (and they are choosing him), he has confused what is coming from *within* him with what is "out there."

So let's talk about the change. It's simple. You're going for *depth*. You want to make a conscious shift in how you're approaching the men you meet—all of them, not just the ones you're interested in. Start by making an effort to talk to men you previously wouldn't have spoken to. This is good for a couple of reasons. First, when you don't want anything from a guy, it's easier to focus on who he is as a person. Second, as you get used to talking to men without any underlying agenda, you will find yourself noticing more of each individual man's *qualities*—ways that he is, and characteristics he has or doesn't have.

Really *listen* to what a guy is saying to you. Regardless of what he is talking about, you will hear a lot about his character. How does he see the world? What are his beliefs about life? Who does he think he is, and what does he feel is his purpose on the planet? It cannot be overstated: character is the most important thing you're looking for in a man. After the potbelly has arrived, the wrinkles show up, and the super-hot sex phase passes, a guy's character is what you will be left with. So it better be good.

Getting into this habit will impact the ways you interact with men you actually *are* interested in. Instead of looking at them in terms of whether or not you want them, you'll begin to think more about who they might be on the inside. Ask yourself questions: Who was this guy in seventh grade? What did he hope to become? What is his deepest wish for his life, and am I a person who could be part of that journey with him?

As you begin to bring more caring—more depth—to your dealings with men, not only will you begin to see something different in them, but they will begin to see something different in you. It comes down to the energy you are putting out there, which will always, and I mean *always,* return back exactly what you sent out. It's like a boomerang. If you send out deep, you will get back deep.

No matter what the qualities you think you're looking for in a mate, I can guarantee you that what you really want is super simple: You want love. You want peace. You want a happy, harmonious partnership with a person who also wants that and is capable of creating it with you.

What the Last Guy You Dated Knew but Couldn't Tell You

So after reading Chapter 2, you know why that awesome guy only took you on one date. Let's go over it once more, to recap:

- **You're shallow.** You're focusing on superficial things and not paying enough attention to what's important—like a man's character.
- **It's perfectionism.** That's what shallow really is. You treat men like objects who are going to complete you or your life in some way. Good men see this from a mile away and will avoid you.
- **Grow up.** Shallowness comes from thinking like a teenage girl, who is way too concerned with what other people think.
- **Let go of your list.** You're not looking for what you want anymore. You're looking for what you need.
- **Go deeper.** Look at the *person* inside the man. See what motivates him, find out what his life journey is about, and really ask yourself if it's something you would feel good being a part of.

3. You're a Slut

Or, Why Casual Sex Probably Won't Get You Married

1. Do you regularly have sex with men who aren't committed to you?
2. Do you find yourself getting hooked on men you only intended to have casual sex with?
3. Do you feel like sex with a partner is the only sex that really counts?

LET'S BE CLEAR: you can have sex with whomever you want. I truly don't care what people do with their bodies in private—I'm not here to moralize. However, your sexual behavior is obviously a component of your overall dating and mating picture. When I talk to a woman about her partnership story, one of the first things I ask about is sex. When do you have sex with a new partner? What do you do during the in-between times? Do you try to maintain friends with benefits? Does it work? How is your sex life with yourself? How, when, and with whom you have sex is going to impact your potential for marriage in a number of ways.

Being a slut is just one of those ways. Now, I know "slut" is a provocative word. And I don't really mean that being promiscuous is a bad thing, per se. I mean, as long as you're treating your dear self well, who's to judge? But having sex with men you are not committed to, or who are not committed to you, can be problematic in ways that you can't just *think* yourself out of. Especially when it comes to getting married.

There is a biology underlying sex and dating and mating that is, in most cases, bigger than the really cool idea that you should simply be able to have sex with a guy and keep it fun and light. In theory, that's possible. In practice, it rarely works. (I know a grand total of two women who can do it successfully.) As I am fond of saying, casual sex is like recreational heroin—it doesn't stay recreational for long. Sex, especially good sex, is habit-forming. And because of that, it can seriously get in the way of creating the kind of relationship that leads to marriage.

What It's Really About

What I'm talking about is *casual sex*. And what I mean by that is any sex outside a committed relationship. You have no idea how much I hate that I sound like a conservative politician here— because I'm so, so, so *not*—but in my thirty years of dating and talking with women about their relationships, I have come to a similar conclusion, though for totally different reasons. I'm not saying you have to put yourself on ice completely, but if you're the kind of woman who finds herself embroiled in sexual relationships that aren't leading you to marriage *and you want to be married,* you are going to want to rethink your approach to sex.

Casual sex is probably the biggest lie ever. Sex is never casual. It's always going to be a thing that brings babies into the world, builds kingdoms and destroys them, and causes people to kill their spouses. The fact that there was a whole decade, from the Summer of Love (1967) through the Summer of Sam (1977), where people successfully fucked whomever they wanted whenever they wanted has done much to confuse modern sexuality. We just had the bad luck to have it depicted in such cool music, movies, and television that we were able to convince ourselves it could happen for us, too.

It's important to note that all casual sex is not created equal. There are different types of casual sex: the kind you set out to have, the kind you settle for, and the kind you don't even know you're having because the guy hasn't told you that he's not really in a committed relationship with you. In fact, there are as many kinds of casual sex as there are guys who only want to sex you casually. Here are a few of the most common types you're likely to run across:

- *The cad.* This is the rogue who delights in acquiring the affections of interesting, beautiful women and who will dissemble, misrepresent, or prevaricate in order to get them. He probably won't point-blank lie about getting into a relationship with you, but he will certainly let you lie to yourself. This guy tends to be found in certain professions that give him access to lots of beautiful women—like fashion photographer, bartender, or advertising executive.
- *The Peter Pan.* This is the guy who can't get serious about you because he can't get serious about himself. He's running around town on a skateboard, looking super cute in his thrift store outfit. You'll find yourself making excuses to your friends for his three roommates, his smoking and drinking, and his job at the coffeehouse. The only thing he's on time for is band practice. You keep hoping he'll decide to grow up, but face it—it's never gonna happen, at least not on your shift.
- *The career builder.* Some guys are so focused on their ca-

reers, they just don't have the energy to put into a relationship. Women love career builders because they're eligible—they look an awful lot like husband material because they work hard, oftentimes are well educated, and frequently can be found in well-paying professions. But make no mistake: a guy who wants to put everything into his career can take *years* of your life if you let him. The redeeming quality of this guy is that he's usually up-front about where he is and is just looking for women who are okay with it. He will commit someday, but not to you unless you're still thirty-one when he makes senior vice president. Which isn't going to happen, because you're thirty-one *now*.

- **The cheater.** This is the guy who can't commit to you because he's committed to someone else—in the worst possible way. What can you say about this guy, except that if you're into him, you probably have work to do in therapy about your dad? Other versions include the guy who's getting all emotionally close to you—like a BFF—but without any sex because he is, after all, in a relationship with his actual girlfriend. And then there's the guy who's seeing you because he's *this close* to getting out of his relationship with the wife or girlfriend he's still living with. It should be a total no-brainer, but if a guy is in any way tied up emotionally with another woman, leave him alone.

- **The intriguer.** This is the guy who loves your attention so much, he tantalizingly dangles the prospect of a relationship in front of your face, but never seems to actually deliver. He calls or texts or runs into you *just* enough to keep you interested without ever actually making any promises. He's a little like the ad copy on a zillion-dollar cosmetic cream: worded so carefully that you can't really say what he promised, but you just know he gave you the distinct impression it was going to be *amazing.* And, oh, the jar the cream comes in? Gorgeous. He's super ultra frustrating because often there is a woman he *is* willing to commit to—it's just not you. It's some dangerously beautiful girl who plays drums in a rock band. Or something like that.

- ***The Jack Nicholson.*** Last but not least, there's the guy who is *never* going to commit. Ever. But his rakish charm keeps you from caring! He might have money, sex appeal, or humor, but in any case he is just plain funner than other men, partly because he's unencumbered by thoughts that wear other guys down—thoughts of anyone but himself! If there's any one of these types you're going to fool around with, he's probably your safest bet, because none but the *most* delusional girl even thinks for a moment she's going to get Jack Nicholson to settle down. That, and he's also *old.*

It's worth noting that none of these guys are *bad* guys. They are just motivated by their own self-interest, and they are at a place in their lives where self-interest means staying open to more than one woman. Nothing wrong with that. Unless you're trying to (1) get them to change or (2) wait them out.

If either one of those is the case, you might be waiting a long time. I can hardly think of a girl I know who *hasn't* given up months (or years) of her life hooked on some guy she was trying to have a casual relationship with. It seems to get more pronounced as a woman gets older, but it happens at every age.

Why Melissa's Not Married

My friend Melissa is one of the more extreme examples of this phenomenon. She started dating a super-handsome French guy

Not Necessarily Better Living
Through Chemistry

The process of bonding and falling in love is part of a whole system designed to get us hooked on a guy long enough to get a baby with him. There are these chemicals that help the process along: oxytocin, dopamine, serotonin. Those chemicals feel *good*. They produce the sensation of being "in love"—actually, at one level, they *are* the feeling of being in love. If you didn't have the chemicals, you wouldn't feel the love.

Before I knew about the biology of pair bonding, I thought there was something *wrong* with me. How come I couldn't figure out how to just boink a guy and move on? It looked like everyone—at least on TV and in movies—was doing it without a care in the world. Everyone except me. I always started *wanting* the guy. Loser.

I wasted years trying unsuccessfully to have casual sex. I grew up in the 1970s and fully expected that when I turned eighteen or so, I would be having lots of sex. Casually. I saw *Saturday Night Fever* the summer before eighth grade, and I couldn't wait. New York! Dancing! Outfits! I was super psyched to get with Tony Manero and have sex outside the club in the back of Double J's car.

But that's not what happened.

What happened is that I made out with a guy toward the end of tenth grade and ended up in a two-and-a-half-year relationship with him. And when that ended, I made out with another guy and ended up *marrying* him. After five years we split up, and the next guy I made out with, I stayed with for a year. And so it went. If I got sexually involved with a guy—and I mean even a couple of big makeout sessions— I'd end up bonded to him. I didn't end up marrying all of them. I didn't even end up in relationships with all of them. But I sure did end up bonding to them.

Which is why—when the chemicals naturally recede eighteen to twenty-four months into a relationship—some people (and by some people, I mean my former self) feel like they're no longer "in love" and think that means they're supposed to leave the relationship for a different one in which they will feel "in love" again. They don't know that "in love" is basically a chemical state. They're thinking it's related to *the person.*

It isn't. Not necessarily.

named Pascal in her early thirties. For the first four months, things appeared to be unfolding in the usual manner. Pascal wasn't necessarily promising a long-term relationship, but he had some nice pillow talk, he called her *"Chérie,"* and he definitely didn't say anything to rule it out, either. The trouble started when the relationship would have begun to hit the customary let's-go-deeper-into-this-thing milestones—turning points like having a toothbrush at the other person's house, sharing a holiday, or meeting the parents. Let's put it this way: for Melissa, those points never turned.

By the time nine months had passed with no real progress in the relationship, Melissa had figured it out—Pascal had no intention of committing. So she broke it off. Or tried to. Not surprisingly, after a month or so they started "missing" each other. A few bouts of drunk-dialing later, Melissa decided to try another tack. Why not just keep it casual? After all, she liked him, she didn't have any prospects she was more interested in at the moment, and the sex was incredible. So, yeah. *Why not?*

Because that was nine years ago. That's why.

Melissa has dated a ton of guys in that time, some she really liked, but she keeps going back to Pascal. Why? No one even comes close to the intimacy, the fun. She's got a history with Pascal. Sure, there's psychology involved—loving an unavailable man, yadda yadda. But on an even deeper, biological level, Melissa stays with Pascal for a much more straightforward reason: she's bonded to him.

Spending years with a guy like Pascal is a little like buying a car without knowing how much it is—because the price will be paid in the years lost to the great sex Melissa is having with Pascal.

Here's what I want to tell Melissa: she may look thirty, but her eggs are forty. I'll say it to you, too: *you only have so many eggs, ladies.* It effing *sucks,* but it's true, and if you want to get married and have kids in that order (not that I'm stuck on the order), you need to take responsibility for this fact ASAP.

The thing is, the whole aging business creeps up gradually. I've seen it happen to at least a half dozen friends. One minute you're going around in your early thirties, dealing with various interesting and sexy men, and the next time you turn around, you're whizzing into your deep thirties. No years of your life will pass more quickly than those from thirty-two to thirty-seven—the difference between "plenty of time" and "OMFG." I'm not trying to be an alarmist. It's just that I've seen so many good women not understand that your thirties are no joke. You might have to get serious pretty early on if you want to start a family without needing to visit the fertility doctor.

Notes from My Life as a Pregnant Bride

I learned this particular lesson by having a near miss myself. I had the stupid luck to get knocked up—by a really nice guy, who was willing to commit—at age thirty-one. This was back in the mid-1990s, before every actress in Hollywood was jumping on the baby bandwagon. I was the first of my friends—at least those living outside of Minnesota—to get pregnant. Believe me, when I announced to my homegirls in New York and L.A. that I was going to be giving birth the next April, everyone looked at me like I was *insane.* But some deep inner voice told me I wanted that baby more than anything else *in the world,* and even though I'd only been dating the father less than six months (and at the time I found out I was pregnant we were, technically, broken up) there was never a moment's question in my mind. Motherhood, here I come—whether the dad wants in on it or not.

But of course the dad wanted in. Because, after three years of living in New York—a town where I was in absolutely no danger of being committed to (committed, maybe, but not committed *to*)—I had resolved to date only guys who would truly be with me. That meant dating "good" men, even if that good man wasn't the kind of guy who would have grabbed my attention while gallivanting down Avenue A in the East Village.

Looking back, this was the smartest thing I ever did. Not that I take particular credit for it. I feel like this is one of those lessons you learn when the person in front of you gets in the car accident that you just barely miss. At heart, I know I am exactly the same

as my girlfriends who have found themselves unmarried and un-
pregnant at forty-one; I have all the same thoughts and feelings
they do. It's just that, owing to my terrible childhood, I was never
really secure enough to date and have sex casually.

It's also important to let you know that I wasn't sure about dating that good guy. At the time I was more than a bit torn—should
I hold out for a hipster dude, the kind who *doesn't* wear overalls to
a big Hollywood party at Adam Sandler's house? (True story.) Ultimately I went with my higher instinct, chose goodness over cool,
and learned a very valuable lesson: there are more important
things in life than what a guy wears to a big Hollywood party.
(Actually, there are more important things in life than big Hollywood parties.) I know because I'm now fifteen years into my ex-
marriage with Mr. Overalls and he's just as high-integrity a person
today as he was then.

Okay, so the takeaway is not that the earlier you start dating
good men, the sooner you can accidentally get pregnant and marry
one. But it could be.

Some Relevant Stuff About Men

You'd think we all know this by now, but men do not fall in love
through their penises. They just don't. The vast majority of men
can happily fuck strangers and buddies alike and have no problems keeping those relationships right where they want them:
over there, on simmer. Maybe that's because they're better at
compartmentalizing, or maybe it's because they don't have as
much oxytocin as we do, but the reasons don't actually matter, do
they? The important thing to know is that no amount of great sex
is going to turn a dude into your man if he doesn't want to be.

For many, if not most, men, getting into a long-term relationship is a *decision*. They may be having all the same intense feelings as you are, but a healthy man doesn't exactly fall in love. It's more like he makes a clear-eyed assessment of the real potential of the relationship, and if he likes what he sees, he decides to allow himself to "fall" by letting go some. Then, as things develop, he lets go some more, then some more, then still more— until he is all the way in the relationship. The letting go progresses as he discovers who you are—if you can be trusted, if you're sane, if the sex is good, if he thinks he'll like what life would be with you, and most important: IF HE'S READY.

Sometimes it's hard to tell whether the relationship you're in is just slow to get off the ground or whether the guy is simply having casual sex with you. A lot of the behaviors look the same—at least in the early stages. But here's the difference: you will know if a man is deciding to fall for you, because he will tell you so.

If a guy you are seeing regularly and having sex with regularly doesn't tell you he is falling for you in the first month or two, you can pretty much assume he isn't. And if you're still wondering— because we ladies do like to hold out some hope—there is a foolproof way to find out: if you have to ask if you're in a relationship with a guy, *you aren't*.

Then there is a more confusing situation, where the guy is in a relationship with you but it's just not very deep. This is what's happening for my friend Erica. She's been seeing a guy in his forties for the past seven months. Erica and Tony spend every weekend together and a couple of nights a week. Tony has three kids and an ex-wife, who apparently take up so much room on his hard drive that he really just wants to have a low-key relationship with Erica. Actually, Tony may say "low-key," but in practice, what he really means is "casual." Because even though Tony is monogamous, employed, a homeowner, and when he's got free time happily spends it with Erica, he's not truly available, because the relationship is not really going deeper. Erica is very tentative about bringing up their future together—a red flag, since the future is pretty much off-limits in a casual relationship—probably because at heart, she knows there really isn't a future much beyond what they have right now.

Erica wants to wait to discuss a lifetime together until Tony's children are older and his ex-wife will be a little less of a daily part of his life. But it won't really make a difference. Because the truth is, having kids and an ex-wife isn't something that keeps a man who wants to go deeper into a relationship from doing so—if he wants to. Tony just doesn't want to. That's a fact that Erica would rather not have to confront just yet. And who can blame her? No one wants to give up a man they love.

How You're Going to Have to Change

Number one: *stop dealing with unavailable men.* Nothing will keep you single against your will the way staying involved with unavailable men will.

That's why, if you're looking to marry in the near future, I cannot urge you enough to be very mindful of whom you bond with. As I said, I could start having sex with, like, Quasimodo and next thing you know, I'd be wanting him to propose. In fact, I've always thought another interpretation of the Beauty and the Beast story is that it *doesn't actually matter* if the guy I'm with is ugly or awful—if you give me some high-quality sex, I am going to attach to the guy no matter what. Unfortunate, but apparently true.

So if you're interested in marriage, you want to think about hopping into bed with someone the same way you would consider a boat that you wanted to use to sail across the Pacific Ocean.

Are All the Good Men Taken?

Definitely not. But recent research offers a clue as to why it might seem that way. Apparently, lots of women find men who are already in a relationship way more attractive than men who aren't.

Social psychologists at Oklahoma State University showed subjects a photograph of an attractive person of the opposite sex. Half the people in the experiment were told that the person was already involved with someone else, and the other half were told they were single.

The outcome was telling. To people already in relationships, it didn't significantly matter whether the person in the photograph was single or attached. But that wasn't true of the single women in the study—they showed an overwhelming preference for men who were attached. When told the man in the photo was available, 59 percent were interested in pursuing him. And when told he was already in a relationship? A whopping 90 percent of single women said they wanted to go for it.

There is a term for this phenomenon: mate poaching. And though researchers in this study theorize it's possible attached men are more attractive to single women because they've already shown they're willing to commit, evolutionary biologists say one thing is clear: mate poaching is really just one of many human mating strategies—and sometimes a very effective one. Just look at legendary Hollywood mate poachers like Elizabeth Taylor and Angelina Jolie.

You'd make sure that boat is seaworthy, right? It better not have any major leaks, giant holes in the sail, or busted navigation equipment. Same with a man. You're not looking for perfection; every man on the planet has flaws. What you're looking for are the baseline qualities of a good person—kindness, humor, honesty— and the key, a willingness to commit. You don't even have to be sure just yet that the guy wants to commit to *you*, but he does have to be willing to commit to *somebody*, somewhere. And if he has a track record of commitment, even better.

Because one thing I know for sure is that you are not going to turn a guy who doesn't want to commit into a guy who does. This is so important, I'm going to say it again:

> *You are not going to turn a guy who doesn't want to*
> *commit into a guy who does.*

If unavailable men are an issue for you, this may be the most important thing you take away from this book. Even if you do manage to get the guy into some kind of liaison with you, at best you will just be turning him into a liar (see Chapter 5). And at worst, you will be turning him into your punching bag—because you *will* end up blaming him for not committing to you.

Number two: *take care with yourself.* Sometimes a man can be the source of great advice on love. This happened to me recently. I was visiting Rome, where a very old friend from college now lives. I hadn't seen him in twenty years at least. We went to lunch and caught up on our lives. Including, of course, our romantic lives.

It had been a while since I'd gotten out of my last relationship, and actually, I was fine with it. Almost shockingly fine. Like, multiple cats fine. I had started to worry a little—after all, I'm the girl who's been married three times! Relationships are super important to me, and I never thought a day would come where I wouldn't care one way or the other if I was in one. Anyway, after a really nice lunch, a walk through a-*mazing* Rome, and a stop at a gelato place *(sigh)*, my friend said to me: "Tracy, you are a very captivating woman. Just don't settle."

I should say that this is coming from a former English professor who now works in one of the world's most exciting professions—he's a film producer—in one of the world's most beautiful and romantic cities. Not that I was falling in love with him, because for starters, he lives half a world away, and for enders, he used to be married to a really good friend of mine. But still, this is a guy you would definitely listen to if he told you that you were captivating and that you definitely shouldn't settle.

Don't settle. It's great advice. The issue is that these two words are often misconstrued to mean going for, and getting, everything on a list you might have been compiling since sixth grade. That's not what my friend meant. What he meant is that I am worth being committed to (which I know) and by someone who really deserves me (which I don't always know). He meant that I need to take care with me, the way I would take care with something I really valued. It's a message that I need to take to heart. Because when it seems like a guy is offering me something, I'm often tempted to just take it. Other times I'm tempted to just leave it. Either way, I lose sight of the real question: is this the *right* thing for me?

Spiritual Stuff That Will Help You Change

There is a spiritual mechanism in life where sometimes you have to let go of something so-so in order to make room for something awesome. Yes, we've all heard stories about the girl who is languishing in some not-so-great relationship when the fantastic thing just comes up and taps her on the shoulder. But more often, it happens that you have to consciously let go of what you don't want in order to signal to the universe that you're ready for the thing you do want.

Which brings me to the next thing I'm going to tell you to do that you might not like. I want you to *stop filling up empty space* in your life with guys who aren't going to be your man. Let the empty space be empty. Yes, it will be painful. You might be bored or feel alone. But by committing yourself to a committed relationship, you will be setting the stage for a whole new level of man.

The biggest reason I see that we women hang out with guys we'd never marry is that we're lonely and we want to feel something (or at least something better) right now. But you can't put a new car in the garage when the old one is still in there. Maybe you're so wrapped up in Mr. Not the Guy that you can't even *see* Mr. the Guy. (Or he can't see you.) Or maybe you've come to a point where it's less uncomfortable to stay in the kind of relationship that isn't working than it is to let go of it. Either way, you have to assume that if you were going to meet your "real" man while you were keeping company with the "fake" ones, it would have happened by now. Unless you want to rip a few more pages off the calendar while you persist in the idea that maybe . . . *maybe* . . . you will.

Recently I was part of a panel discussion on love and relationships. Also on the panel was a thirty-nine-year-old woman who wants to be married. As happens at these things, a twenty-seven-year-old woman in the audience stood up and said, "No offense to the unmarried lady on the panel, but I have no intention of being single at thirty-nine."

I pointed out that few women *intend* to be thirty-nine and single. It just happens. Or rather, it just happens when you spend lots of time on men who have no intentions toward you. So if you are in a relationship where you hear yourself saying any of the following—

- I'm just doing this until he figures out how awesome I am and commits.
- I'm just doing this until something better comes along.
- I'm just doing this until (fill in the blank).

—you should probably let that relationship go. This is not a dress rehearsal—this is your life. You're only going to get one time around. Make it good!

When your mind starts telling you it's unfair that you have to be alone when everyone else is out there enjoying fun sex and the good feelings that go with it, remind yourself that you are committing to yourself—your own plan for your life—so that eventually someone will commit to you. After all, if you don't find yourself worth committing to, why should anyone else?

As for what to do in the meantime, I have a radical suggestion: develop a sexual relationship with yourself that is as awesome as anything you have with a man. Because that's the other big reason you're keeping those non-committing-type guys around, aren't you? You want to have sex. I get it, sex feels good. But here's what I have to say about this: *you are awesome in bed—even if you are all by yourself.*

Let's talk about being alone. First of all, I can tell you that you can absolutely get to a place where you feel happy and fulfilled and *fine* on your own. And when you're in that place, you are going to be attracting a whole different type of man. The big downside to being alone: no peen. I'm not saying there's no sex, because there can still be sex. Sex is everywhere! It is an energy that exists all over the place. Most important, it is *within* you. So I want you to go in there and find it.

I know lots of women who feel like the sex they're having with themselves is second best. This simply does not have to be true. Okay, so maybe there's no penetration—though if that's your thing, that can be remedied, too. I know it sounds so cheesy, but you can make love to yourself. Seriously. It's about bringing to *yourself* the spirit of being turned on, of being into it, of being every single thing you want a man to be for you. And about bringing to *yourself* all the feelings you want a man to create in you.

This can be much more challenging than it sounds. Ultimately, it will test your self-esteem. How dependent are you on a man? Can you support yourself sexually? Is sex something you bring to a relationship or something you take out of it? You may think you're having sex because you're horny, but chances are high that if you think the only "real" sex is the kind you have with another person, there is some sneaky psychological stuff going on there. Like, you want validation. And a woman who is dependent on validation from men is not excellent wife material.

I want to suggest that you develop a sexual *relationship* with yourself that means as much to you as one you would have with a man. That way, when the man does come along, he joins a party that is already in progress—he's not the very first guest.

This is a challenge to the way many women think. They tell me it's "just not the same" with themselves as it is with a man. Of course it's not. But if partner sex is your only definition of sex, you are stuck having to acquire something (or in this case, someone) in order to experience your sexuality. Not only is that false, it's also unworkable.

There is a profound shift that happens when you view yourself most of the time as a woman who is a whole sexual being, right now—and that is a shift from sexual object to sexual subject. *Your* experience of you becomes more important to you than *their* experience of you. And when that happens, you will no longer be willing to settle for just any old warm body, whether it's a committed relationship or not.

Because from a spiritual standpoint, remember: you will attract what you are. And when you are loving yourself on every level, you are already acting as a match for your perfect mate.

What Your Sister Knows but Hasn't Told You

So let's summarize what we've covered in Chapter 3:

- *You're a slut.* You're having—or trying to have—casual sex with people who aren't committed to you, and even though it might still feel good, it's no longer working for your bigger life goals of marriage and children.
- *Casual sex is a really big lie.* Not only because you have hormones that are going to bond you to someone you're having sex with, but also because sex makes people do crazy things, like marry a teenager or abdicate the throne.
- *Men don't fall in love through their peens.* Most of them could have sex with you for a thousand years and it would never produce the feeling of being "in love"—unless they had that feeling to begin with. For most of them, getting into a long-term relationship is a decision. Period.
- *Stop dealing with unavailable men.* You won't move forward in this area until you do. Because you'll never convert a guy who doesn't want a commitment with you into a guy who does. You just won't.

- ***Let there be emptiness.*** Instead of filling up your mind, life, and bed with a man who isn't committed to you, be alive to sex wherever it is. Go dancing. Take a kundalini yoga class. Touch a man's arm. All these things will ground you in your sexuality in a much more powerful way than having sex with a guy who doesn't want to be in a relationship with you.

- ***Love yourself.*** The sexual relationship you have with yourself is the building block of every other sexual relationship you have. Make it good.

4. You're Crazy
Or, Deal with Your Inner Courtney Love

1. Are you the kind of person who's always got some drama going on?
2. Have you ever hurt someone, something, or yourself in a fight with a man?
3. Do you sometimes suffer consequences from things you said or did impulsively?

HERE'S YOU BEING CRAZY: You're in New York with your new boyfriend. On vacation, your first together. As you walk into a restaurant you're squabbling over something minor, or at least something that *should* be minor. But as you sit down at the table his phone buzzes—two short blasts, which you know is a text, not an email, because you pay attention to stuff like that—and he checks the message. You watch him poke at his phone and this *feeling* roars through your chest. You definitely know better, but you're still pissed about the squabbling thing, so you decide to damn the torpedoes. A moment later, there you are, asking the one question no woman in the smartphone age should ever ask: "Who's that?"

He's pissed about the squabbling, too, and besides, this relationship just started, and he can't let you think you can control him like that. So he looks at you and says the one word no woman in the smartphone age ever wants to hear: "Nobody."

The words on the menu are all scrambled and your mind is doing a monologue: *This guy seriously doesn't get me. He's probably cheating. I'm never going to get my needs met here. He's definitely cheating. I shouldn't be in this relationship.* Over and over. You know you're supposed to be cool—but you're just *not*.

When your boyfriend asks if you're upset, you shake your head, because if you say anything, it's going to be obvious that you're freaking out over a text message, and you know that's not okay. Your heart starts beating even faster, and you're getting that tight, fearful feeling in your chest. When he presses you—"What's wrong?"—he sounds slightly annoyed, and you feel so judged you can't stand it another second, and all of a sudden it's like, *That does it.* You get up and walk out of the restaurant.

That'll show him.

For one second you *love* knowing that he is sitting in there all by himself, looking stupid and, you hope, feeling terrible, right in front of all those hot New York women. You focus on how wrong it was for him to sound annoyed. You remind yourself that you really don't want to be in a relationship with someone who makes you feel that way. Even if all relationships are relationships that make you feel that way.

But now that you're standing out here on the sidewalk and he is coming toward you, you can see that your plan may have worked, but only for thirty seconds. From the look on his face you have obviously done serious, possibly irreparable damage. Your new man—the man you love and want to be with—is looking at you in the worst way a guy can look at you . . .

Like you're crazy.

What It's Really About

Crazy is about *intensity*. It's about being out of control emotionally; acting against your own best interests in your relationships;
stoking lots of drama; being needy, easily hurt, jealous, insecure,
and/or in other psychological states of being that men are not
looking for in the mother of their children. It also includes eating
disorders, crying after sex, and anything you can easily picture
Courtney Love doing.

Intensity is when a regular relationship feels boring to you.
You're looking for something more along the lines of Sid and
Nancy, but without the murder. Movies, television, and love songs
insist that intensity equals love. It doesn't. It equals chaos. Think
of Elizabeth Taylor and Richard Burton in *Who's Afraid of Virginia Woolf?* Do they really have to ask who's afraid? The answer
is Virginia's husband, her co-workers, her mother, and everyone
else she knows.

Crazy comes in two basic flavors: major crazy and minor crazy.
If you're major crazy, you already know it, because you have been
told so by at least three people who aren't even among your exes.
Major crazy involves major actions—like the girl I know who
threw a Duraflame log into the front seat of her ex-boyfriend's new
car and set it on fire. Violence, self-harm, serious vandalism, and
destroying someone's reputation (even if it was your own) all fall
into this category. Major crazy is never cute or dramatic if you're
a danger to yourself or others.

Minor crazy is more subtle. Think of stuff you've said and done
in your dealings with men that caused you to break out in the
WTFs. Like my friend Suzanne. She'd been seeing this super-
cute guy on her daily run around a local lake. Over the past couple of months they'd moved from eye contact to sunshiny hellos as

they passed each other. As the flirtation grew more consistent, Suzanne naturally started hoping it might go to the next level. Then, one weekend, she got her highlights done. But oops, they're way too blond. Like, Gwen Stefani blond, which, in Suzanne's words, made it look like she was wearing a wig.

Obviously, slightly-too-blond highlights are not a bona fide life problem, but here's how Suzanne's mind works. Now she doesn't want to see the guy on the trail. It's not a big thought, but it's there: *he's not going to like me.* And so she skips the trail until she gets the highlights fixed.

That, folks, is minor crazy.

The easiest way to tell if you're crazy is if you are constantly telling long, involved stories about what happened this past weekend. You might even have a team of very special (i.e., co-dependent) friends who love to live vicariously through your drama. That's the thing about intensity: it's addictive, and it loves an audience.

That's why the first thing you will have to do is stop talking about it. The high you get by replaying the intensity through re-telling the story to your ten favorite co-dependents is almost as good as the high you get from all the drama in the first place. And your co-dependents have to get back to work, anyway.

The fact that you have co-dependents stowing away on your crazy train points out what is really going on with romantic insanity, whether major or minor. And that is *dependency.* If you look closely, the cray-cray comes out of an underlying belief that we are dependent on the outcome of what happens with a given man, and we're not going to be okay unless things turn out a certain way (usually the way where we get what we want: the guy).

Please note: hardly anyone *consciously* believes they want a guy that bad. Most of us pretend to ourselves that we're fine—

Intensity Is a Bigger Deal for Men

Intensity is not the same for men as it is for women. Psychologist John Gottman has done a lot of research on what happens when men and women interact with each other—whether it's simply talking to each other or full-on fighting. Gottman coined the term "flooding" to describe what happens when adrenaline gets pumping and the fight-or-flight reaction is triggered. The pulse races, blood pressure rises, muscles tense, and the heart thumps almost painfully. What's interesting is that Gottman found men become flooded more often and more easily than women do. And once flooded, people find it impossible to think logically, act rationally, or focus on what their partner is saying.

This explains the differential between what men and women consider to be "negativity." What we ladies consider fairly harmless—the Kenny G of complaining, criticism, or fighting—may be experienced by a man as something closer to Metallica live in concert.

It's also why you need to handle your crazy. Because men aren't kidding when they say they just can't handle it. It's scientifically proven that they can't.

fine—whether we get him or not. But that might not be true. Often the belief that we won't be okay without him lurks—like the craziness itself—below the level of awareness.

If you break down your behavior, though, you can see it pretty clearly. Why would you text a guy nineteen times because he failed to answer your first three texts? *Because you're not okay until you hear back from him.* Why would you vandalize his property because he broke up with you? *Because he has taken something from you that you don't want to live without: himself.* Why would you still be fantasizing about a guy you broke up with months or years ago? *Because deep down you're not sure you're ever going to find anyone better.*

It's all sort of circular: reducing the craziness is about loosening the dependency, and when you loosen the dependency you will lessen the intensity. And with the intensity gone, you might find something you never expected: *calmness.* Which could freak you out. Because when things get quiet in a relationship that has been very intense, it's uncomfortable. Neither partner quite knows what to do with all the peace! Suddenly there's all this time for *relating*—you and your boyfriend feel so close! And maybe you don't even really like it. Which is when you discover what all that intensity has been doing for you: ensuring that your relationships never get too intimate.

Notes from My Life as a Jealous and Fearful Girlfriend

I figured this out—and by figured out, I mean a boyfriend helpfully yelled it at me during a fight—about five months into a new relationship. I was doing my usual jealous and fearful routine (because that's how I was way back in, oh, the early 2000s—okay, maybe it was closer to 2010 or 2011) where I express all kinds of "intuitions" that my boyfriend is going to leave me, if not now, then sometime in the next twenty years.

My solution to that fear is to go all Sherlock Holmes on a guy. Not that I snoop through his phone or email (I mean, not without serious probable cause). I'm more subtle than that. No, I root around in his psychology, searching for clues from his behavior in past relationships, his childhood, his relationship with his mother. I interpret those clues. Then I present my "evidence" that he will inevitably abandon me—which somehow always sounds exactly like criticism. Naturally, boyfriends don't like this. They tell me I'm crazy and retreat. Which I use as proof that I was right.

Over the years, I performed this lovely little cycle from about the time I really started to fall for a guy until I got more settled in the relationship (like, while cutting the cake). But the particular boyfriend mentioned above was especially perceptive, and one day, right in the middle of a big row, he said to me: "Don't you see what you're doing, Tracy? You're just pushing me away." And then he said in an I'm-mad-as-hell-and-I'm-not-going-to-take-it-anymore tone of voice: *"Stop it."*

For whatever reason, probably my advanced age, I suddenly *got it*. The light went on and I saw how I'd spent my whole adult life fighting with men as a way of getting them to back off. Because when a guy is close to me, I like it, and when I like it, I fear it will be taken away. So I just push the guy away before he can abandon me—which creates the exact outcome I fear, but at least I am "in control" of it, right?

Uhhhh, *right*. Which is, in a word, crazy.

Some Relevant Stuff About Men

Few boyfriends would have handled such a situation the way that one did. Because nothing freaks guys out like when you're being crazy. It makes them feel turned off and weird—and that's when you only break out in some craziness once in a while. If it happens regularly, they feel victimized, frightened, and angry. The only guys who are going to desire a long-term partnership with a woman who makes them feel like that are the ones with the moms who are bananas. And God bless 'em, those guys have enough to deal with already. Besides, we don't really need any more weirded-out, victimized, frightened, or angry men out there. It's bad for them and it's bad for us. It's bad for the world.

The reason guys don't like seeing our craziness is that, intuitively, they know it's a sign of dependency. It means you have somehow put too much emphasis on this guy, this situation, and how it turns out. And that scares them. I visualize dependency as a person leaning against something, like a table. If the table suddenly moves, what happens? You fall over. No healthy guy really wants you to be that kind of dependent on him. It feels too much like you might do something drastic if he ever leaves you, or even if he just wants to do something girls hate, like attend a bachelor party or have coffee with his ex-girlfriend.

By the time they hit thirty, most men have had at least one bad experience with a crazy girlfriend and therefore are more adept at spotting it in you than you might be at spotting it in yourself. Just know that if you have had a lot of guys call you crazy or say you're just too intense, this is what they're talking about.

My dude friend Tommy recently ended a situation like this. In the late 1990s, Tommy briefly dated a smart, compelling Australian actress named Jane. They had this intense love affair that ended abruptly because Tommy was in his early thirties and at least ten years away from even *thinking* about settling down. (In Los Angeles and New York, guys usually lag at least seven years behind their chronological age.) Jane was heartbroken but eventually moved on.

Fast-forward to 2011: Tommy and Jane reconnect. Now that they're in their forties, it's no less hot and intense—in fact, it might be even more so. They sleep together on the first night, and for the next two months the house is on fire. But the deeper they go into the relationship, the crazier Jane becomes. She starts getting really emotional after sex, bombarding Tommy with her fears. She remembers how Tommy left her the first time, and she's terrified it's going to happen again.

As time goes on, Tommy not surprisingly starts to distance himself—which, not surprisingly, only ratchets up Jane's fear even more. What Jane should do is dial back her relationship with Tommy to a level that she can comfortably maintain. But she's gotten minorish crazy, so instead of letting go a little more, she *hangs on* a little more. Uh-oh. Soon she's so emotionally overextended that when Tommy fails to call the day after they burn the house down once again, Jane goes over to his house on a Sunday and flips out—all while Tommy is minding his own business fixing his carburetor.

In short, Jane has re-created exactly the scenario she's worried about. Why? Because she went deeper into the relationship than she was able to go *while still staying emotionally comfortable.* Let's say having sex with a guy takes a certain amount of funds in your emotional bank account. Jane was spending with Tommy way past what she could emotionally afford. When you see this happen, you have to dial back. But instead, Jane tried to turn to Tommy for reassurance—to "make up the difference" between how deeply she was invested in the relationship and the amount of funding she had in her emotional bank account. What happened? You guessed it—Tommy, feeling overwhelmed by Jane's need and the craziness that it caused, abruptly ended the relationship again. A very predictable reaction for a guy.

Why Lauren's Not Married

My friend Lauren has another quality men love (*not*): she is possibly the most impulsive girl on the planet. Actually, she has that very special combination of low self-esteem and impulsiveness that causes her to kill her relationships, using her cell phone as a semiautomatic weapon.

For example, Lauren's most recent dating situation ended with her sending *nineteen* text messages over the course of one insane all-nighter—capped off by a 6:40 a.m. phone call telling his voice mail it was *over*. By three o'clock the next afternoon she wanted to take it all back, but the guy—wisely—never picked up the phone. To make matters worse, she works with the guy, so now she has to see him from time to time in the elevator. To say things are awkward is to understate it by a factor of about a thousand.

Writing vitriolic, emotional, or intense texts and emails is like playing Russian roulette, except all the chambers are loaded but one. There might be a teeny-tiny chance that the impulsive thing you feel you absolutely must say right this second is going to have a positive effect on the relationship, but that chance is too small to warrant the risk. I tell Lauren that if she absolutely must write angry emails and texts, go ahead, but (1) observe a strict twenty-four-hour rule before actually sending anything, (2) have a trusted friend who reads all your emails *before* you send them to their intended recipients, and, most important, (3) do *not* put the recipient's name in the "to" line until *after* you have read the message to your impartial someone—you don't want to "accidentally" send it to the person in question.

So how do you know if it's okay to communicate something to someone? Well, I have a pretty foolproof method for determining what needs to be done or said at any given moment in time: *if you have an urge to do something, don't do it.* Generally speaking, an urge is a signal that you have temporarily lost your mind. And the stronger the urge, the longer it's going to take you to find your sanity again. Urges let you know that you are absolutely, positively dealing with a feeling or thought that is emotional in nature. And if you're viewing a situation through your emotions, you're seeing the most skewed version possible. You need to let the intensity subside and come back to it when you're seeing a little less neon and a little more sepia. Again, if you must talk about it, call a friend. Nine times out of ten, after about twenty minutes the urge will probably have passed.

It's too late for Lauren's work guy, but taking these kinds of precautions might go a long way toward saving her future relationships—*if* she combines techniques like this with an attack on the underlying issues.

How You're Going to Have to Change

You're going to have to *get help.* Obviously I'm not a therapist, but I have spent thousands of dollars with one (or six). I've also read about seventy books hoping to unlock the mysteries of my own dysfunction, and I'm happy to say it worked! I now know that most of the insane bullshit I've been doing in relationships is related to my childhood. Talk about insight.

You can be pretty sure your insanity is related to your childhood, too. If your craziness is keeping the husbands away, the question is really one of degree: is your stuff major or minor?

If you've done major crazy stuff more than once in the fairly recent past (say, one to three years), you have only one choice: get major help. You need to go to therapy immediately and start dealing with the childhood trauma that almost surely underlies such acts. The part of your mind that tells you you're not *really* that fucked up is lying to you. That doesn't make you a bad person, but it does mean that as soon as you get into a relationship that triggers you in a specific way, all those feelings—and thus all that crazy behavior—will come roaring back like a yeast infection where you only took the medication for two days.

If you think you can't go to therapy because money is an issue, it's not. Pretty much every county in America has mental health resources available at low cost. And lots of therapists dedicate a portion of their practice to people who pay on a sliding scale. If you want it bad enough, you will find it. Just pretend you're stalking your last guy's new girlfriend on Facebook.

If you're more into the minor crazy stuff, you still have things from childhood to deal with before you can create a healthy relationship, but maybe it's more like a barbeque than a four-alarm fire. Start by dealing with the dependency that the cray-cray can't exist without. There is more to life than a guy—whether it's any guy or a certain guy that you are totally into. I know you know this, but sometimes, when you really break down what you think about and talk about during a day, it appears suspiciously like what you really believe is that your life won't start until you meet your life partner. This just isn't true.

You've heard a million times that you need to be a scintillating, interesting, fascinating person if you want to attract the perfect life partner. What I'm suggesting is that you want to be a scintillating, interesting, fascinating person so you don't bore yourself to death by making men way too important in your life. Because as soon as you get that man and you've had him for a while, you're going to realize he's not all that—no man is!—and you're going to want to have something else to do.

The solution, as one of my wisest therapists used to say, is to come home to Tracy. (Put your name where mine is.) At first this just sounded sappy and lame. What in holy heck does "Come home to Tracy" mean? So I sat there a minute and imagined myself walking in the door to my house. Not the one I was living in at the time, but the one I saw in the Jennifer Aniston issue of *Architectural Digest*. I imagined myself coming home to a plush mid-century with perfect light and a sparkling pool. I imagined how happy I would be to hang out there. What would I be doing?

And that's when I realized that, after therapy (and all that it entails), what you need is *hobbies*. Lots of them. Hobbies may seem too simple to be worth talking about in a book about relationships, but they're not. Because hobbies are all about *you*. They are about your passion. Who are you? What makes you *you*? How do you spend time with yourself and build your relationship with yourself? Your hobbies are special time between you and you. Like the Big Sister/Little Sister program, except this time you're both the pretty career lady *and* the disadvantaged girl with the big eyes and the pigtails.

So think about what you *love* to do. (Besides him.) Start doing it. That way, when he doesn't call, or decides he can't commit, or realizes he'd rather chase after an unavailable woman than be with someone who is right in front of him, you can return to a big pile of *you*. With activities you love. Because you love you in a verb way, not just the feeling way.

For me, that is writing, gardening, knitting, music, reading, and going to the movies. It's also talking to my friends, going for walks, cooking something yummy, fixing something around the house, checking out a museum, watching a great TV show, and having a wonderful cup of coffee. Think about what you did as a kid or teenager when you were so bored you couldn't take it. What were your go-to activities? For me it was a brand-new book or magazine—I could sit down with it and escape, in a good way, into another world. And I'd learn something in the process.

I'll never forget the moment I figured out just how sane I had become. I had gotten into a fight with a boyfriend, and he had left in a huff. Rather than feeling panicky and calling him repeatedly or running after him, I simply looked around and said to myself, *Oh, cool. Now I can spend some time working on the essay I was writing.* I didn't lose a minute's sleep that night. And when I woke up in the morning, he was at my front door with a Hallmark card, coffee, and a pastry.

Coming home to Tracy, indeed.

Spiritual Stuff That Will Help You Change

From a spiritual standpoint, your craziness is where your wounds are—whether they are wounds from childhood or those from past relationships. It's where you don't believe you will be supported. Where you fear that if you don't do something, *no one will.* It's where you store, or metabolize, your pain over life's hurts and disappointments. The good news is that dealing with your craziness will set you free in all areas of your life.

The antidote to being crazy is to know that you have *choices.* As mentioned earlier, when you are being intense, dependent, and out of control, it's like a tantrum—you have reverted to a childhood state. There's a saying that children who grow up in dysfunctional homes don't have any power and know it, while adults who live in dysfunctional homes have power and don't know it. Leaving the craziness behind is about understanding that you have power—you just need to exercise it in a way that works *for* you, not against you.

Choices help you shape your story. Like we talked about in

Chapter 1, the things you tell yourself are going to have a major effect on how you relate to men and relationships. At the bottom of every crazy thing you do is a story that casts you in a victim role. And who wants to marry a victim?

There is a term for getting yourself through the moments where the crazy surfaces: "self-soothing." Probably no psychological or behavioral skill is more important to having a great relationship than this one. Self-soothing is just what it sounds like: it's where you gently take yourself by the hand and calmly walk yourself out of the department store of life when you're on the floor kicking and screaming. It's when you know how to take ten deep breaths before you make that phone call or do something impulsive. It's anytime you have to tell yourself everything's going to be okay and force yourself to come up with some genuinely believable reasons for why that is so. ("Because Oprah said so"? Sure, if it works.) Sometimes, for me, self-soothing is as simple as letting the shot clock run out on a bad day—getting to eleven o'clock so I can get in bed, go to sleep, and know that when I wake up, I can start fresh.

In fact, the whole choices/self-soothing thing is about *getting some control over your mind.* New thinking is something you work your way into, rather than something you can put on your credit card. Here are three big areas where I see a lot of women get stuck in their thinking:

1. *Your real man can never "get away."* You need to commit to a thought pattern where nothing in your love life is happening by accident. If a guy leaves, *no matter what the details are,* it's only for one reason: *because he's not your man.* Even if he says some mean shit on the way out, like your eyebrows are too bushy or he doesn't like the way you sing. You have choices. So you're choos-

ing to *know* that his bushy-eyebrow problem is really just the universe's way of getting him out of your bed so that your real man can get in there. Knowing this will help you move on much more quickly, and without turning into a big pile of Poor Me. Instead of having to figure out why it didn't work each and every time the thought of him pops into your mind, you can just move straight to "He definitely wasn't it," because if he was, he would be here.

2. *You are going to have a great life, no matter what.* It's very important that you *choose* to believe you're living in a world where it's inevitable that you will have a great life. This is your responsibility! You can't expect to sit around thinking victim thoughts and have a great relationship just show up and beg you to get in it. If your heart is set on having a marriage, you must believe you will have a marriage. Not because you will "get" a marriage, but because you will *choose* to be in a place where a marriage can happen. This means you prepare yourself. You have to be a wife before you can get a husband. And if you're crazy, you're not yet a wife.

3. *Hold the pose.* You know how in yoga, the teacher asks you to get in a pose, and at first you're like, "Shoot, I got this," and then forty-five seconds later you're freaking out, wondering when in hell it's going to be *over*? That's what the process of making choices is like.

Every time you choose to know—and it has to be *know*, not hope—that your most wonderful man can find you *no matter what the odds look like right this second,* you will be moving toward your (im)perfect marriage. But it might not happen in the first month, or even the seventh. It *will* happen, though, if you keep choosing what you *want* over what you *don't want.* Not an easy task.

However, as you do this choosing, over and over—first for one day, then for another day, then for a week, then for a month, and eventually automatically—you will soon find that you have regained a lot of the power over the way your mind moves through its emotional landscape, especially when it comes to relationships. Soon you will notice that you feel different, and soon after that your life will start popping out, and up, and over, in new and exciting ways.

What Your Cubicle-Mate Knows but Hasn't Told You

So let's summarize what we've covered in Chapter 4:

- ***You're crazy.*** You thrive on intensity and being emotionally out of control, and that's just not what most guys are looking for in a life partner.
- ***Crazy freaks men out.*** They feel victimized and frightened by it unless their mom was nuts, in which case they have enough problems without you adding to them.
- ***Get help.*** Childhood stuff is like crud that builds up on the inside of the lid of a jar. If there's too much, you won't be able to open the jar. Therapy helps you clean that stuff out.
- ***Get some hobbies.*** Join a band; take up ice skating. Hobbies are where you build your relationship with yourself, which takes your dependence on a relationship with a man down a notch. And it's your dependence on men that's causing you to act crazy.

5. You're Selfish

Or, Marriage Is About Giving Something, Not Getting It

> 1. Is your picture of marriage mostly about the house, the baby, or the financial security?
> 2. Are you the kind of girl who rotates through jobs, men, people, and apartments?
> 3. Do you think of a relationship as an opportunity to serve another person?

IF YOU'RE SINGLE, CHANCES ARE you think a lot about you. You think about your thighs, your outfits, your nasolabial folds. You think about your career, or if you don't have one, you think about becoming a yoga teacher. Sometimes you think about how marrying a wealthy guy—or at least a guy with a really, really good job—would solve all your problems. You know that saying about how it's your world and the rest of us are just living in it? That's how you feel!

Sometimes you secretly wonder if you even need a spouse. Maybe you're just fine on your own. I mean, who really wants to deal with another person all the time? Other people suck, frankly. They get in the way of eating cereal for dinner or applying your cream hair remover in the middle of a Saturday afternoon. They're always lying on the couch watching something you don't like on TV and eating something that smells disgusting unless you're the one eating it. You have to clean up after them. Perhaps if you could have a spouse who lived in the house next door—actually, maybe more like a block or two over—that would be perfect. They'd be there, and yet they wouldn't be there.

This sounds pretty good, doesn't it? Be honest. It does, right? I mean, if you're American, you're pretty much born feeling like this. 'Cause we live in *the most selfishest country in the world.* This is a country built on individualism and the pursuit of happiness. We're so individual and so happy that around 46 percent of all households are maintained by a single person. That's some fifty-two million single people, none of whom are traveling in the car-pool lane of life. And at the moment, you're one of them.

But lately you've been thinking you might be ready to leave all that behind. And you can. Right after you stop being so self-centered.

What It's Really About

Selfishness is exactly what it sounds like. It's when you approach men (and, really, the world, but this is a book about relationships, so let's just focus on that) in terms of *yourself*—how they make you feel, how they make you look, what they'll bring to your life or what they won't. You might say, "Well, duh, is there any other way to think about men?" Believe it or not, there is. But we'll get to that.

Selfishness makes people act like children, who want what they want when they want it. Children are egocentric. They think the world revolves around them, and they can't see how their actions affect others. Or they can see it, but they can't feel it, or they don't care. This is why being selfish makes partnership impossible. Because you can't partner with a child. You can only take care of one.

But if you're selfish, you *love* being taken care of. In fact, you're pretty sure someone should be bringing you a venti mochachino right this minute. After all, you deserve it. If you're wondering what selfish looks like, just think of any diva-like celebrity. (Actually, pretty much any celebrity will do.) If your behavior in any way resembles asking someone to do something for you even though you can't be bothered to look them in the eye, you are probably selfish. If you want someone to put the title "Miss" before your first name—even if it's an *invisible* "Miss"—you are probably selfish. If you feel like you would be great on a reality show, you are absolutely, positively, most certainly selfish.

Another reason selfish people make lame spouses is because they do not play well with others. Most of their actions are directed toward getting what they want, keeping what they have, or getting rid of what they have that they don't want. (Like best friends, jobs, apartments, and, sad to say, people.) As you can imagine, this is no fun for their partners. Because when a selfish person has no more use for you, you're out of there.

Men who have been to the rodeo a few times know this. Pretty much all of them have encountered a selfish woman at least once in their dating lives and gotten burned. From that point forward, guys might be willing to put up with a selfish girl (and by put up with, I mean fuck her) as long as they think they won't have to deal with her for life. But they are naturally wary of marrying such a woman, not only because selfish people are nearly impossible to make happy—and guys do not want to live with someone who can't be happy—but also for a much more basic reason: because a selfish person makes a bad parent.

For this reason, selfishness will interfere much more with your mating than with your dating. A selfish girl can usually find a guy to be with her for a while, but he won't want to pull the trigger on the relationship.

Here's a quick list of some other ways you might be practicing selfishness without even knowing it:

1. *You're rigid.* This used to be known in the olden days as being set in your ways. It was commonly thought to be a thing that prevented old maids (of thirty-six) from finding mates. And they were right. When you need every single thing to be exactly the way you like it, you have to know that there are not a lot of men who are going to find that attractive. It's okay if the pillows on the sofa are out of place, and it's okay if the toilet seat is up. Get over it.

2. *You're ego-driven and/or materialistic.* If your main orientation toward a guy is whether he's going to make you look good, buy you stuff, or pay off your student loans, you are thinking way too much about yourself. You cannot possibly expect another person to do something for you that you are, technically at least, capable of doing for yourself. Which is a long way of saying: get a job.

3. *You're needy.* No one ever thinks they're needy. They just think they're looking for a little bit more of whatever it is they want from whomever it is they want it from. If you're needy, it means you see yourself as a person who should be on the receiving end of most transactions. This is an unrealistic expectation, to say the least, in the context of marriage. If you're wondering if

you're needy, take note of your next five phone conversations. If the other person ends them more than 50 percent of the time, the answer is I'm afraid so.

4. *You can't self-soothe.* You have no way to calm yourself down when you don't get what you want. So you go shopping or drinking or eating, and if all that fails, you take out your frustration on the people around you. If you have a man in your life, you expect him to talk things over with you until you feel better, even if that takes three or four hours. And by talking, I mean he sits there listening to you. Note: if you can't self-soothe, you'll know, because you'll get the feeling that everyone thinks you're really special, but no one will tell you why. Really, they're just afraid of you.

5. *You want to sit in the window seat (or the aisle seat, or the seat facing the door) every time.* This one is so obvious it should go without mentioning—except to a selfish person. No one gets their way all the time. You know that, right? But you'd be surprised. Because there are lots of chicks out there who really think part of a man's job is to absorb discomfort for them. Yes, there is a long history of chivalry to base that on, but in practice, it's just not fair. Or grown-up. At a certain point, it really begins to feel a little more like a daddy-daughter dynamic, and if you think about it, that's just weird. So if you're doing this, stop.

If any of this is pissing you off, there is probably something here you need to take a look at before you are ready to be carried over a threshold. Chances are good, though, that if you've ever been in a long-term relationship, someone has pointed it out to you already. You just need to know that selfishness is like a stowaway—it hides in so many attitudes and behaviors, you sometimes have to look really closely to see it.

Why Jenny's Not Married

Take my friend Jenny. Her selfishness shows up as being *judg-mental*. Jenny is thirty-five, very pretty, sweet, and eager to have a baby—but her self-centered quotient is off the chart. I can't tell you how many times I've heard her say in a somewhat impatient tone: "I don't know if I *want* to be with a person who [fill in the blank]." I feel like saying to her, "But *everyone* is a person who fills in the blank about *something*. Even you!" Does she think *she* should get left over that thing, or rejected as a partner because of that thing? I hope not.

Jenny's selfishness also manifests as her being *unrealistic*. Quite often she is mad at someone who isn't doing what she wants them to be doing. She doesn't realize that other people aren't doing what she wants them to be doing because *they're just people* and they've got their own shit that they're reacting to and dealing with. She seems to think they should be reacting to and dealing with hers. Clearly, in her mind, other people are not so much autonomous human beings as extras in the movie starring her. This level of selfishness is making it hard for her to sustain a relationship.

Take, for example, the guy Jenny dated last year. They were together three or four months and he really liked her. The guy, Doug, was divorced and had one child, but he was open to having more. He wasn't perfect, but he was gainfully employed, owned his own home, and was nice-looking. Their dating was not very eventful, which is to say nothing really went wrong—which can be a very good start to something. They had nice conversations and better-than-decent sex, and he wanted to take things to the next level. But Jenny just couldn't stop being critical of Doug— she didn't *quite* like the way he dressed, talked, decorated his house, or made his money.

Now, normally I would tell a girl to pay attention to her feelings, because the body can be a great barometer of what is really going on in a relationship. (For instance, if your body tells you a guy is cheating, he very well might be.) But in this case, nothing Jenny said indicated the presence of a true deal breaker. After several months of dithering, she finally broke it off.

Now it's a year later. Recently we were talking about men, and while Jenny was recalling her relationship with Doug and the reasons for its demise, she said: "I mean, he used to bite his nails." It was like an alarm went off in my head: *this is why she's not married.*

Here's the thing: you can leave a man for a lot of things, *but nail-biting is not one of them.* And while there are almost certainly more reasons than his ragged manicure that made Jenny jump ship, the fact that she even mentions it is indicative of a kind of mercilessly critical thinking toward men that is so self-centered, it's shocking. It's petty, and when you're leaving guys for petty stuff, you are going to end up alone. Because it doesn't matter which man you're with—you're going to find something wrong with him. You can be sure of that.

Notes from My Life as the Mother of a Baby Man

I had a nice long love affair with selfishness. It lasted about ten years, from roughly right after my rotten childhood up until the period where I was thirty, living in New York, and couldn't get a boyfriend. Which forced me to start taking a good look at myself.

Until that dry patch (okay, so it was more like a dry *field*), I had had a string of long-suffering men who had valiantly put up with me. At the time I thought it was cute to be badly behaved (I seriously did think that), but when I look back, I realize that those guys had the patience of Mother Teresa. Or maybe it was the co-dependency of Mother Teresa. Either way, with me as their girl-friend (or wife), they were on the "give" side of give-and-take.

Because nowhere did my selfishness show up more than in my dealings with men. I acted as though men existed to meet my needs. I wanted a guy to give me time, attention, sex, conversa-tion, time, attention, sex, conversation, and more time, in that order. I didn't really want a boyfriend; I wanted a hostage who was also an umbrella holder. And I didn't even know it. If you had asked me, I'd have told you what a great—no, *great*—girlfriend I was. Of course I thought that. I was full of myself.

Then the universe played a big trick on me—it gave me a *baby*. And not just a baby, but a baby boy. *A baby man!* What? Little did I know I was about to go to Dude School, with a double major in Guy Studies and Getting Over Myself.

In short order, my life became about doing things I didn't par-ticularly want to do (feed someone) when I didn't particularly want to do them (the middle of the night). I also had to carry heavy things while carrying squirming things, as well as be at someone's beck and call twenty-four hours a day. *And* clean up vomit.

The shocking thing is that I rose to the challenge. It's as though I were living in my own little movie montage, set to some fun mid-tempo song you'd hear on The Coffee House on satellite radio. There I am whipping up homemade baby food. And single-handedly unfolding a stroller so complicated it probably had its origins in the space program. And so what if I'm picking a lint-covered pacifier out of the sofa cushions and popping it into my baby's mouth? The montage ends with me saying, "What vomit?" I'm now a really nice lady who knows how to care about someone other than myself.

I firmly believe this is why you see a lot of celebrity women get husbands after they adopt. The kids put the woman on notice: *Bitch, hello! It's not all about you anymore!* And after she's spent a year or two of thinking about someone other than herself, suddenly Brad Pitt or Harrison Ford comes along and decides to significantly other her.

Inside every husband is a baby man. And when you learn how to love that little guy, you're hitting graduate-level Dude School.

Some Relevant Stuff About Men

As my son continued to grow, I came to the realization that he was the single-cell version of the men I had encountered in my years of sailing the Man Sea. What an epiphany! I suddenly saw how most of the behaviors I had gazed upon from a place of self-centeredness—like, "Why isn't he talking to me, or calling me, or thinking about me, or doing what I want him to do?"—had nothing to do with me! Can you imagine? I hadn't really considered that.

Kind of a Tool

At one point in my life, I realized that I treated men the way a tool treats women. Just like the most selfish men, I divided the opposite sex into two camps: (a) those I wanted to date and (b) those I didn't. Those in the latter group were invisible. Then, when I had a boyfriend or husband, either (a) they were doing what I wanted or (b) they weren't. I essentially viewed men through the prism of my *self*, my ego—and I always found myself superior, which is the essence of chauvinism. I evaluated them, and valued them, on the basis of how well they worked for me. As if they didn't exist for any other reason.

I'm not saying this is what you're doing with men. Still, this point of view—that a man's worth was somehow tied to his value to me personally—was so embedded in my life, I couldn't even see it. I'd always been really clear about how lame it is when, say, a male boss wants a pretty secretary. But I didn't even know the extent to which I held a similar attitude: men who pleased me existed, and the men who didn't please me didn't exist.

As the mother of a boy, I now see that there are significant challenges to growing up male. Sexism really does go both ways—men don't *actually* have it better than we do, unless you think growing up in a world where you are expected to have no feelings and die in wars and have an average life expectancy that is five years shorter is really better. As a woman, I would like to see what happens if we commit to being more loving and less adversarial with men. What if it starts with me? I truly believe this is the next chapter of feminism. To put down the sword and pick up the . . . I don't know, backscratcher?

Furthermore, I was never going to change those behaviors. Nor did they really need changing. Dudes, even the ones who can talk about their feelings, have a different way of moving through the world. Part of it is physiological—their brains are different from ours, and so are their nervous systems—and part of it is psychological, which is another way of saying *they're guys*.

At the end of the day, I'm really sort of French. Gender studies be damned, but I don't believe it's all just a construct. Men and women are not the same. And if you've been part of a kids' play group, you know what I mean—a disturbing percentage of the time boys like trucks and girls like princesses. Even when their parents eat organic. And I've finally come to accept that. *Vive la différence!*

Which brings me to my big takeaway: generally speaking, the men in my life weren't holding out on me; *they were just like that.* They were giving me what they had, when they had it. And not giving it to me when they didn't have it. It was rare (to the point of never) that they had what I wanted but were simply refusing to give it to me. They just weren't. In fact, nothing has made me less selfish with men than committing to the idea that most people (men, women, everyone) are doing what they can at any given moment in time. If they're not doing it, it's because they *can't,* not because they won't. So I can just stop punishing everyone for not being able to respond to my (mostly selfish) list of demands.

For years, I'd been proceeding on the theory that most of the things men did were learned behavior and all I had to do was "teach" them out of it. To be perfectly honest (and this is embarrassing), I didn't even think their male way of being in the world was valid. I thought the woman's way—of talking through things, of processing emotions, of emotionally relating—was superior. And I was very presumptuous about it, too. It never occurred to me that asking a man to talk to me, dammit, could be more or less the same as a man asking a woman to stop being so emotional.

There's even a word for what I lacked: respect. Learning respect changed the way I related to men in a very basic way: I got off their case and started seeing them for who they were. It should have been obvious that I couldn't sustain a healthy partnership with someone if I couldn't even respect them, but that's what self-ishness is—a lack of respect for other people. It's saying, "Me, my thoughts, and my feelings are more important than yours, so they should come first." No one wants to marry someone who approaches love in this way, because that isn't really love.

How You're Going to Have to Change

You're going to have to *be a better person.* You know how there are people who are just naturally "good people"—they're helpful, courteous, thoughtful, gracious, polite, and kind? In other words, super annoying to a selfish person? Well, you're going to have to be like that. Except for you, it's not going to come naturally. However, there is a secret shortcut that will take you from where you are now to where you want to be in one move—kind of like Chutes and Ladders, without having to roll a 6. And the shortcut is: *stop living life through your feelings.*

Just stop.

Most of the time, your feelings are not what you think they are. They are not super-precious babies that need to be nurtured and protected and cared for. You do not need to walk around with them strapped to your chest in a BabyBjörn with their legs dangling. You can do that once a week in therapy for a fifty-minute hour, but that's it. Because your feelings are not all they're cracked up to be.

In fact, living your life through your feelings is a surefire way to ensure that you are thinking about yourself *all the time.* That you stay selfish. Yes, sometimes your feelings are important—

when there's a death in the family, when something really big happens (good or bad), or when you are grieving your childhood trauma. But like I said, there's a time and a place for that.

The rest of the time, your feelings are not more important than getting out of bed in the morning, going to work, asking after someone's family, or changing your tampon. And they're definitely not more important than anyone else's feelings. If you want to have a happy life—and certainly if you want to have a loving relationship—you have to put your feelings in their proper place.

I know a great way to take the focus off your feelings: quit paying so much attention to them. On days when my feelings are acting up, I treat them like they are unruly customers in the returns line at Ikea and I am the beleaguered clerk. While my feelings are demanding to speak to the manager, I simply stay calm and try not to escalate things. "Yes, ma'am," I say to them. "I see you, and I hear you. Now please have a seat and I'll be with you just as soon as I can." (I put the emphasis on "soon," so my feelings know I really do care about them, I'm just not prepared to stop everything and let them cut in line on *my whole fucking day*.)

My feelings *hate* this! They start jumping up and down in the background like junior-high kids in a TV news live shot. But your live shot is a great relationship and you can't let your feelings ruin it. A well-developed man is not going to get deeply involved with a selfish woman who allows her feelings to dominate her world. It's just too exhausting! No self-respecting man wants to live in that kind of (avoidable) crisis.

And, frankly, do you?

Spiritual Stuff That Will Help You Change

The spiritual remedy to selfishness is *service*. Service is what marriage is all about. Yep. That's what I said: *service*. I want you to serve your husband—and, for that matter, everyone else around you. You will be a much happier person. I'm not suggesting you turn yourself into some sort of maid or geisha. I'm saying you need to step into the idea that loving someone is about giving something, not getting it. (This is equally true for both women and men.) And the thing you're going to give is *love*. Even when someone doesn't "deserve" it.

It's one of the great paradoxes that everyone wants to be loved unconditionally, but no one wants to become a better person than they are right now. This is why there are so many problems in the world of relationships! Everyone wants to stay the same while the other person changes. If you want to be a grounded woman ready to love a real man, *you are going to have to go first.*

And you can start right here, in your regular life. For example, next time you're in the car, let the driver trying to get into your lane cut in front of you. Smile and wave and be nice about it. Feel magnanimous. Notice how much you hate that feeling. This is why you begin with strangers—because at first, being the bigger person hurts. No one tells you that being magnanimous is painful. Especially when you're doing it for your significant other, it feels like someone is getting power over you, and there's a part of you that is going to want to kill them.

It's like trying to get your size 8 foot into a really cute pair of size 6½ shoes. Think about it this way: if someone told you you would be wearing these shoes to the Oscars, you would be willing to do it for one night even though it was painful. Right? However, these are special shoes, and the longer you wear them—i.e., the longer you try being a better you (whether or not he becomes a better him; this is just about *you*)—the shoes will magically stretch to accommodate this bigger you. And if you wear those shoes so long that you wear them out, you will probably find your man magically growing into the space you're creating, too.

As a side benefit, this is going to prepare you for motherhood, which, as I mentioned earlier, is really just one long traffic jam where your kid always gets to cut in ahead of you. Occasionally you will get to go first, but you will feel really guilty about it. Or you will have to pay a babysitter $15 an hour for the privilege.

Again, this is all a spiritual practice. Marriage and motherhood are going to be *full* of moments you don't like. And how are you going to *be* in those moments? Childish, throwing tantrums, fearful, hurt, a victim? Or graceful, loving, good-humored, and a blessing to the people around you? Because these qualities are at the core of service. And if you're worried about doing all this work with no one appreciating it or noticing, don't. Because you don't need recognition for any of this. You will most certainly get the only thing you need; there is no way *not* to.

You get to be a better person.

What Your Next-Door Neighbor Knows but Wouldn't Dream of Telling You

So let's recap Chapter 5:

- ***You're selfish.*** You're always thinking about you, and it's really unattractive. Your selfishness is hiding in all kinds of behaviors; find it and cut it out.
- ***Think giving, not getting.*** The sooner you realize this, the sooner you may say to hell with the whole institution of mar-

riage. (Just kidding.) But do remember, men do not exist for you. Stop acting as though they should.

- *Be a better person.* Stop paying so much attention to your feelings. They do not have your best interests in mind, probably because they want you all to themselves.

- *Practice service.* Don't be a martyr, but try to see what you can *bring* to a situation. Especially your relationships. You'll be a lot happier.

6. You're a Mess

Or, You Need to Get Your Shit Together

1. Do you seem to be attracted to—or to attract—guys with major issues?
2. Are you keeping certain behaviors secret from even your closest friends?
3. Looking at your life *right this minute*, would you say you're ready to nurture a man and/or a child?

HERE'S SOMETHING TO THINK ABOUT. Imagine the man of your dreams has been watching you on closed-circuit television for the past thirty-six hours. Without your knowing it, there were cameras in every room of your house, recording everything you've done, and now the guy you've been waiting for all these years is watching it. Every last hour of it.

What is he seeing?

Your messy room? Your secret ice cream binge? Your one-night stand?

And when he's done watching that, he's going to get copies of your credit card bills, your health records, your DMV history, and the receipt from your last trip to the grocery store. He's going to know everything about you: your income, your work evaluations, your tax returns, and what's in your storage space. He might not read your diary, but he won't really have to, because he's there all the time.

Does this freak you out? Because it is, essentially, what marriage is going to be like. Whoever becomes your husband is going to see you when you've got a giant zit on your cheek, is going to be aware of your vaginal yeast infection, and is going to hear you throwing up when you've got the flu. And that's just the stuff that everybody has. What about the stuff you do that you know isn't even normal? Another person is going to have full access to the most intimate routines and details of your life. You might not love this, but you can handle it.

Unless you're a mess.

A mess is just what it sounds like: untidy. Messiness is not something anyone wants in a roommate or a co-worker, much less a spouse. Having a mess along on your life ride is like finding yourself in a Western where somehow Jennifer Jason Leigh in *Single White Female*—or Reese Witherspoon in that pink lawyer-girl movie—has ended up in your covered wagon, and now you're attempting to cross the Rockies with her in tow. In other words, *if you're a mess, you're a drag.*

What It's Really About

Being a mess is about having *issues*. If you've got something going on that you wouldn't—or couldn't—let the man of your dreams see, you can be pretty sure it's at least partially contributing to your singleness. I'm talking about behavioral, emotional, or psychological stuff serious enough that it is standing in the way of your getting married. Maybe you drink a whole bottle of wine every night (leaving an inch and a half in the bottom doesn't count), or eat too much, or are up to your $425 sunglasses in credit card debt. Maybe you have a fucked-up relationship with your mom, a little problem with obsessive cleaning, or a weird sexual twist. Something like that.

It's not that you have to be perfect. You don't. Everyone, as the saying goes, has their something. But some somethings are more deal-breaking than others. Secretly smoking one cigarette a day probably won't kill a relationship. Secretly smoking crack will. The occasional blackjack weekend to Vegas might not do it, but the occasional shoplifting spree will. It all depends on what you've got going on.

There's an easy way to tell if something is affecting your ability to be in a relationship, and that is <u>whether you want to keep it a secret.</u> Getting into a serious relationship, the kind that leads to marriage, requires revealing yourself. If you have something to hide, you're not going to be willing to do that. But rather than admit that, lots of girls would rather just keep choosing men who won't commit, men they don't want to marry, or men who are more effed-up than they are.

Not that you'd be conscious of it, necessarily. It's more like every once in a while, in some moment when you least expected it, you find yourself thinking that when you finally stop doing (fill in the blank) or having a problem with (fill in the blank), maybe then you'll meet the Guy.

These thoughts don't exactly come right out and announce themselves. They're more like catching a fleeting glimpse of your fourth-grade teacher while walking down the street in a strange city. You ask yourself: "Wait, did I just see that?" And your self answers you: "Naw, probably not."

Thoughts like these hide away because no part of your mind really wants to believe that what you're doing is having any far-reaching effects on your life. But I can assure you that if you want to keep something a secret, or if it's occurred to you that your man may not show up until you deal with some particular issue, whatever you're doing is affecting your love life.

The other big clue is if you've ever thought, "I should cut down on the [fill in the blank]." Like I always say, no one ever wants to cut down on the broccoli or is trying to eat it only on weekends. People want to control their usage of things that are, at some level, a problem. So if you're trying to control some behavior, you need to take a closer look at it.

Maybe you tell yourself you are only doing these behaviors until your man comes along. You might even think your man, once he shows up, is going to stop you from doing these behaviors. (Good luck with *that*.) What you don't realize is that any man who wants you while your issues are still in full effect has (most likely interlocking) issues of his own.

This is true even if he isn't explicitly aware of your stuff. People are animals—we have all kinds of intuitive faculties at work, adding up all sorts of stuff about one another. I believe that, on one level, we perceive *everything* about *everyone*. It's how we know we're attracted to someone. Our minds do a trillion little calculations about that thing coming through his eyes, his gestures, and whatever we're picking up off the little hairs on our arms. In an instant we decide we like him, then we act all surprised when he turns out to love Bon Jovi, have an anger problem, and owe a lot of money to the IRS—just like the last guy did.

As I've mentioned, when someone is a match, we can be absolutely, positively sure it's because some part of us is singing a duet with some part of them. And it's probably not going to be at the conscious level:

> *Her:* OMG, you like purple? I like purple, too!
> *Him:* Cool. Let's get into a really intense relationship.

Nope. The things that attract and bond people to you (and you to another person) have way more to do with what is *unconscious* and *unhealed* than what is conscious and totally not a problem. The aspects of your life that you are careful to keep at the edges of your awareness are like the moon acting on the tides—they exert a powerful pull in your relationships.

Of course, the really big deal is this: if you have something to hide, you may *think* you want to meet Mr. Forever, but unconsciously you have a much more immediate objective—*to make sure no one ever gets close enough to discover what you're hiding.* Because that would mean you'd have to *stop* doing whatever it is that you're doing, right? And if you wanted to stop, why wouldn't you have?

Notes from My Life as a Wine-Loving Wake-'n'-Baker

In the ten years between the end of my first marriage and the beginning of my second one—ages twenty-two to thirty-two—I finished college in Salt Lake City; moved to Portland, Oregon; started a TV news career; met, fell in love with, moved in with, and moved out from three live-in boyfriends; spent half a year traveling through Central America; and moved to New York City.

Along the way, I acquired some *really* bad habits. So bad that, by the time I'd lived in New York for three years, I was virtually undatable. I drank way too much and smoked way too much mar-

Is There a Marital Stability Gene for Men?

Researchers at the Karolinska Institute in Stockholm asked more than 550 twins and their partners a series of questions related to their marital happiness, then sampled the men's saliva for DNA. What they found was really intriguing: the more copies the man had of a certain gene variant (known as allele 334), the weaker his bond with his partner.

Comparing men with two copies of the gene variant to men without it revealed something quite interesting: The men who had the variant were found to be twice as likely as the others to have undergone a significant upheaval in an intimate relationship in the preceding year. Equally interesting was what the study showed about this population's wives, who—compared with the wives of men in the control population—reported less satisfaction in their marriages.

The study also found that men with two copies of the variant were twice as likely *not* to marry their partners and mothers of their children as men who had no copies of the variant.

If you're wondering whether you can test a man for this, the answer is yes. Saliva tests for allele 334 are available online. But I don't think you really need a test to know if you're dating a guy with two copies of the allele. Just look at how happy you are with him!

ijuana. I was also pretty seriously out of emotional whack—I can think of at least two friends who got so tired of my tear-filled phone calls that they started regularly letting me go to voice mail.

I thought I was hiding it. And from a distance, I probably did appear to be a lot like your average successful career gal, with an upbeat personality, an interesting job, and a wide social circle. But to the trained eye, it was pretty obvious that my ambition looked like workaholism, my "friends" looked more like drinking buddies, and my upbeat personality was actually sort of manic. But I didn't know that. I thought I was having a great time.

Until I wasn't.

Somewhere around my twenty-ninth birthday, I started to realize that I could not for the life of me seem to attract another relationship. WTF? I'd moved to New York with my Portland boyfriend (who had taken the baton from the Salt Lake City boyfriend I'd moved to Portland with, who'd taken the baton from the Minneapolis boyfriend I'd married and moved to Salt Lake with . . . you get the picture), but since the Portland boyfriend and I had split up (my choice), there had been no one. *Nothing.* Sure, a couple of guys had offered one-night stands, but no one wanted to be my boyfriend, then move in with me, with the eventual goal of marrying me, like I was accustomed to. The baton was now lying useless in a gutter somewhere.

After three years without a relationship, I was *lonely.* And a mess.

Did I think any of this had anything to do with my holy trinity of work, alcohol, and marijuana? Not a thing. In fact, if you had asked me (and a couple of people *had*), I would have said my joints and my cocktails weren't standing in my way. They were making my life bearable until the next life stage showed up.

But every once in a while, this one idea would float to the surface: that in order to be in a relationship, I was going to have to stop doing what I was doing. Needless to say, this was not an idea I particularly liked. So I tried not to pay too much attention to it. My friends Bottle and Baggie did something for me I thought no one else could—they made me feel safe. And when I thought about letting some New York City guy, all fast and edgy and dangerous, into my world, I knew there would be no way I could handle it without my little coping mechanisms.

So I decided that I would give up my ways eventually, but not right now. Long story short, I moved to Los Angeles, and six weeks later I gave up drinking. Within a year I was pregnant and engaged (in that order) to a super-nice guy. I may not be married to him any longer (I take most of the blame for that—he's a really good guy), but I can say without a doubt that he is the best baby daddy a girl with issues could ever want. And it all started when I let go of my really bad habits.

Why Kaley's Not Married

Kaley's a perfect example of a girl whose issues are keeping her single. At thirty-six, she feels ready for the next level of relationship, but her prospects dim—no, they're pretty much *extinguished*—the moment a date sets foot in her apartment. Why? Her place is a *disaster*. There are dishes piled up in the sink, clothes are a foot deep on her bedroom floor, and the sheets haven't been washed in God knows how long. It looks like a college kid's apartment. A boy college kid.

Kaley is, quite literally, a mess.

Seems like a simple problem—just clean it up, right? Actually, though, Kaley's slob situation is like when you get shingles from having a weak immune system—the shingles appear to be the issue, but underneath, there's an even bigger problem that you *can't* see. In Kaley's case, that would be a big, giant debt. Kaley owes at least $57,000 on six different credit cards, and it's running her life. On the outside, she looks perfect, with the nails, the hair, and the designer clothes—but none of it is paid for. She spends her days dodging phone calls from creditors and trying to hide it from even her closest friends. She worries herself sick at night, wondering how she's ever going to get out from under the debt when all she has is her real estate agent's salary.

Meanwhile, Kaley will only date guys she thinks are rich enough to get rid of her problem with the stroke of a pen—another strategy that isn't working. Because even if she could find that guy, she'd have to level with him first about what's going on, and she hasn't been able to do that. So she just keeps falling further behind, and as the interest mounts, so do her worries. It's even gotten to the point where Kaley has stopped dating altogether, because when she did tell one guy the extent of her crushing debt a few months back, he broke up with her. He liked her, but he just wasn't willing to assume that kind of financial liability. And why would he want to? A relationship is hard enough without starting it way in the red.

This doesn't mean that if you have lots of student loans or a mortgage that you're unmarriageable. The key is whether or not the debt is under control and reasonable (like, for a student loan), and Kaley's most certainly isn't.

Some Relevant Stuff About Men

As I said earlier, a man who is ready to commit is looking for someone who is going to be not only his companion but also the mother of his children. Wait, let me say that again, with italics: *the mother of his children.* That means he wants you to be everything his own mom was, but better. Without all the stuff she did that

Men Are Like Cats

My friend Sara tells an amazing story about her wedding day. She was about to walk down the aisle with both her mom *and* her dad when her mom, Eileen, a vivacious blonde who has been married to Sara's dad for forty-two years (and counting), leaned over and whispered in Sara's ear. "I'm going to tell you the secret of a great marriage now," she said.

Of course, Sara was all ears. "What is it?" she asked.

The processional music was just about to begin. There was a long beat before Eileen spoke. Then she took a serious breath.

"The male ego cannot be repaired," said Eileen.

Sara couldn't quite believe her ears. "That's it? *The male ego cannot be repaired.* That's the secret to a great marriage?"

"Yes, it is," Eileen said—without a trace of irony, and clearly still considering herself just as feminist as you please.

Wow.

I know a lot of you might be thinking that's a really lame thing for Eileen to say. At first glance, it might sound like Eileen thinks men are more important than women. Or that women need to make themselves "smaller" so they don't intimidate their men. Or that Eileen is really old-fashioned. But I beg to differ.

What I think Eileen is saying is that a husband is less like a lizard, who can grow a new tail if his gets cut off, than he is like a cat, who can live without a tail but just can't jump and balance and climb the highest tree without one.

You want to be the kind of woman who emboldens her man to climb the highest tree.

And you can't do that if you're a mess.

prevented her from meeting his needs (stuff you can be sure he has totally repressed).

When a guy sees the way you nurture yourself (or not), he knows whether (or not) you are ready for the responsibility of caring for a family. Even if he only knows it unconsciously. And even if, at first, that family consists of only two people—him and you. You have to ask yourself if what a guy would see watching you on closed-circuit TV is going to make him trust that he will have a good life with you, and in particular whether you are going to be able to meet his physical and emotional needs with him as he is now.

In some ways, that's what it really comes down to. We are more important to men from a nurturing standpoint than they are to us. When women want to be nurtured emotionally, we have any one of a half dozen people to choose from: our best friend, our sisters, our second best friend, and in a pinch our former best friend. Men oftentimes have only us. They're not having intimate, soul-baring conversations with the guys at work. So if we've got some big issue standing in the way of our ability to be emotionally, physically, or spiritually available, they know they're going to suffer. "Suffer" is a strong word, but at a very core level, I'm not overstating this a bit. No man is going to willingly sign up for that.

How You're Going to Have to Change

No point in sugarcoating this one. In order to change, *you are going to have to do the one thing you don't want to do.* You already know what this one thing is—it's your issue—and you are avoiding it like crazy. At some level, you even know it's keeping you from partnering with someone. Or at least you suspect it. But you really don't want to admit it. Because admitting it will mean that you have to deal with your issue, and you don't think you can, or maybe you just plain don't want to.

This is a partial list of typical candidates for the one thing you don't want to do: stop drinking, lose weight, get a job, quit your job, break up with someone, file for bankruptcy, forgive your dad (or your baby daddy, or your mom, or your brother), give up weed, stop watching so much TV, go on medication, go off medication, give up the sleeping pills, deal with your eating disorder, stop being a bitch, go deeper with men, quit having casual sex, and all the other stuff mentioned in this book.

Like I said, this is just a partial list. You know what your thing is, if you have one.

Once you're ready to do the one thing you don't want to do, you can get busy tackling the problem. Do everything people do when they have your issue: read everything you can (make sure you look for similarities, not differences; you want to *identify* your problem, not decide you don't have one), go back to the therapy you quit (especially group therapy, so you can see what people look like when they're trying to stay in denial), join a twelve-step group, go to the doctor, cancel the satellite TV, get acupuncture, or call the credit counseling people.

Just don't expect your life to get better immediately. There is a saying that when a person gives up something that wasn't that big a deal, their life gets better. But when they give up something that is big, like an addiction or a compulsive behavior, their life gets worse at first. That's because big issues are structural—you don't realize it, but they can become the walls and floors and roof of your life without your even knowing it.

One thing that having an issue does for you is that it can allow you to run around imagining that if you could just get rid of it, your life would be perfect. But often, once you start to address your major thing, you find that it's masking all these sub-problems—sort of like a life consolidation loan, where all your less serious problems get rolled into one big issue.

For instance, you have a food addiction problem, which has resulted in your being overweight. You know the extra weight is complicating the dating picture, so you resolve to stop eating addictive foods. But once you stop eating the white sugar, white flour, and junk foods, you realize why you did it in the first place—it eased the pain of being lonely, helped manage your mood swings, and curbed your desire to go shopping all the time. Without using food, you now find yourself with a dwindling bank account and a closet full of stuff you plan to wear when the rest of the weight comes off. And *that's* causing pain you deal with by drinking too much. And so on.

Don't despair—this isn't at all unusual. Your life is an ecosystem. If you change one part, especially if it is a major part, it will have an effect on the whole. You will be tempted to give up, to go back to the old way. At least that seemed to sort of work. But I promise you—*promise you*—that if you stick with whatever process you undertake to do the one thing you don't want to do, your life will get better.

And when you doubt this, all you have to do is ask yourself: if that old behavior didn't work for the first thirty-five years of your life, why would it work for the next thirty-five?

Spiritual Stuff That Will Help You Change

The spiritual idea we're dealing with here is *letting go*. Letting go gets a lot of play in the New Age world, but what does it mean? It might sound like giving up, but it's not. It's more like if you had your hand around something, let's say a bird or a butterfly, and you opened your hand. If the bird wanted to fly away, now it could. And if it didn't, it wouldn't. Letting go is the process of *trusting* that if something is not good for you, you will be better off without it. So let it leave.

Giving something up—especially if it's your *thing*—is really hard. I know, because I've done it. But let me offer a little bit of encouragement: *it is so worth it!* The thing is, the hardest part of letting go is in your mind. Your mind thinks it can't live without such-and-such. You know, of course, that you can. But that's just a theory until you start doing it.

For example, I quit smoking about a dozen times before it stuck. Part of that is because I would allow myself to have "just one." Of course, within seventy-two hours "just one" turned into a pack a day. But I had to quit a bunch more times to really *get* that. Then my mind came up with another clever plan—the new thought I had right before I'd light the match would be, *I'll just quit again tomorrow.* But of course, I wouldn't actually stop again for weeks or months. I had to quit another seven times in order to work through that lie. Finally I got so fed up with the smoking, and I was so *ready* to be done with it, that I quit for good. And when my mind started telling me stories about just having one, or quitting again tomorrow, I countered it with what I *knew:* that if I never picked up the cigarette, put it in my mouth, and lit it, I would never have to quit again.

So, finally, I didn't. And what I found out then is that the smoking was making it possible for me to stay comfortable with being stuck. Once I stopped going outside for ten minutes twenty times a day, not only did I have a shitload more time on my hands, but I discovered I was really uncomfortable with a whole bunch of lameness in my life, like my job, my boyfriend, and my lack of creativity. But if I had listened to what my mind had to say—that I couldn't live without my ciggies—I would never have known that. I also never would have changed.

Giving up cigarettes (one of *many* things I have had to give up over the years—including sexy but lame men!) contained a major life lesson for me: no matter what your problem in life is, the answer is always going to involve letting go. Of something. The reason for this is that life is just one long series of letting gos. Infancy. Having your mom make your bed. Your junior high best friend. Your first bike. Your first boyfriend. Your youth.

What's more, as soon as you're done letting go of whatever it is you're being asked to let go of at any particular moment in your life, you're going to have to let go of something else. Then, not too much later, you're going to have to let go of *another* thing. And when you've let go of all kinds of stuff over and over, you're going to have to let go of the one big final thing: your life.

This is not meant to depress you! Rather, it's to say that on a spiritual level, the whole journey of living is about letting go of things—people, places, ideas, opinions, and positions. The more you let go, the freer you become. And the freer you become, the more graceful (and comfortable) your journey through life is— because you're not resisting so strongly.

Understanding this is a big part of being a mature woman in a relationship. Knowing how to let go allows you to deal thoughtfully and compassionately with arguments, disappointments, and hurts. Since you've cultivated an awareness of the big picture—that, ultimately, your whole life is about letting go—it's not such a big deal that you have a husband who is stubborn or arrogant or in denial, or whatever else he's doing that's human.

Viewed another way, what we are calling your "issues" are really just attempts to protect yourself against this one big undeniable truth of life: that when all is said and done, no one is keeping *anything* around here. What better way to guard against the pain of losing something than just not to get it in the first place? Shoot, Shakespeare asked that question a few hundred years ago: *is it better to have loved and lost than never to have loved at all?*

At a core level, your issues protect you from the pain of loving and losing. But once you see your behaviors for what they are—strategies designed to avoid having to be truly vulnerable to another human being—and once you see that being vulnerable is unavoidable, you become willing to just let go. Ultimately, letting go is about expanding. It's about being free.

Let the change happen. Let the life happen.

What Your Sister Would Tell You if Only She Knew What Was Going On

So let's summarize what we've covered in Chapter 6:

- *You're a mess.* You have issues, and they need to be handled before you can successfully partner with someone.
- *You're keeping a secret.* This is how you know something is a problem for you. No one's hiding how much broccoli they eat.

Not that the whole world has to know everything about you, but if you don't want your *sister* to know something, it's probably something that you're not really okay with, either.

- ***Do the one thing you don't want to do.*** Chances are you already know what you've got going on that is standing in the way of your relationship. Let go of it. It might hurt, but it will only be temporary. Staying the same will hurt forever.

- ***Letting go is ultimately what life is about.*** Your issues are really about trying to protect yourself from the risk of loving someone. Letting go means setting yourself free. Let it happen!

7. You Hate Yourself

Or, You Can Only Love a Man as Much as You Love Yourself

1. Is there a running commentary in your mind that compares yourself—favorably *or* unfavorably—with others?
2. Have you sabotaged things you dearly wanted—seemingly against your will?
3. When people talk about self-love, do you wonder what they mean?

SELF-HATE IS STEALTH. It doesn't come out in a long, sparkly gown, stand in the spotlight backed by a many-pieced orchestra, and sing a song to you about how much you don't like yourself. Not at all. Self-hate is more of a trickster. It glides through your mind all camouflaged, like one of those really genius frogs in a nature documentary that look *just like* the tree they are sitting on. You don't even see the little guy until he blinks, and even then only if you are looking *verrrry* carefully.

Another way to think of self-hate is as a virus—say, the herpes simplex virus—where you don't even know you have it until there's a giant, hideous scab on your lip. At first you can't believe this is happening to you—you're not really a cold sore *person*—

but there it is, right on your lip. Your response is to just pray for it to hurry up and go away, and when it does, you very conveniently totally forget it ever happened . . . until one day it comes back. You again express surprise because, like I said, you're not really a cold sore *person*—despite the proof right on your face that you obviously are.

That's how self-hate is.

Self-hate is just lying dormant below the surface coursing through your bloodstream unseen until it surfaces in some effed-up situation in your life. Then it comes out in a blaze of glory—or is it a hail of bullets?—showing up mostly as a running monologue that is so familiar, you don't even hear it most of the time.

Self-hate is the part of you that is telling you that your life will never work, you'll never be happy, that everyone else got the life manual so they know what's going on, but you didn't, so you don't, because clearly you're a loser—and by the way, you're fat. That is, unless it's telling you how much *better* you are than everyone else. Because sometimes self-hate would rather project its ugliness onto other people.

When the self-h8er talks—and self-hate is chattier than that lady sitting next to you on a cross-country flight—it sounds so *real*. Even when it's not talking, it's just down there, invisible, exerting this really gnarly influence on your love life. Without you even knowing it. And until you deal with it, it will absolutely, positively, for sure keep you single.

What It's Really About

Self-hate is really about *not being good enough*. It's not that you *actually* aren't good enough. It's that the self-hating part of you wants you to believe you aren't, and it's got some very crafty ways of convincing you. Why would it want this? Well, that's complicated. Psychology has some pretty good explanations involving an internalized parent or some reenactment of childhood trauma, but really, all you want is to move forward in your life, and is a psychological theory going to help you do that?

What's going to help you right this minute is to understand that self-hate is cunning. Mostly you walk around thinking you're absolutely worthy and deserving of everything you want—you just can't figure out why this stuff you're deserving of never materializes the way it does for, say, Gwyneth.

But it's also more perplexing than that, because self-hate often surfaces when *the thing you want is right within your reach.* You start dating a good new guy, you lose seven of those last ten pounds, you're next in line for a promotion at work—and suddenly there's this low-level hum of negativity. You're sure this thing you're *so* close to having, the thing you thought you were so ready for, is going to go away. Self-hate starts its sabotage. You find yourself being irrationally jealous right in front of the new boyfriend, eating french fries for a third day in a row, or arriving to work late *again* and hoping no one notices. You know doing these things is bad and you wish you weren't doing them, but there you are, doing them anyway.

Self-hate is a *destroyer.* A big N-O to everything you want.

Self-hate is also a shape-shifter. And one of its favorite ways to present itself is through the idea that *nothing is good enough for you.* This is when you reject people and things that *could* make you truly happy, in favor of people and things that will satisfy the self-hate. For instance, you decide to stay on unemployment and wait for your dream job instead of accepting a decent-but-can't-immediately-see-how-it's-going-to-get-you-the-career-you-want job that will let you support yourself and your kid. Or you decide to skip a friend's birthday dinner in order to hang out with a guy who has a girlfriend but likes to practice bad boundaries with you. Or you keep trying to make coffee dates with the super-busy girl you want to be your next BFF—even though she's never, ever available. Then you end up feeling bad.

Self-hate loves to talk you into these kinds of choices because, at the end of the day, it knows you will conclude—once again—that you suck and you will never have enough money, be loved, or have great friends. Because the key way self-hate operates is that it tries to get you to do things that will *prove what it believes about you.* The net effect is that you feel you're not good enough and never will be. As a result, you stay where you are instead of moving forward in your life. And perhaps the biggest way you are staying where you are is that you never quite find the relationship you want.

Why Jasmine's Not Married

Jasmine is a really nice girl. Pleasant-looking, friendly, with a wide smile, a big heart and a bubbly personality—she's got what it takes to make a kick-ass wife. But first she's got to understand that she's good enough, because right now she really doesn't. If you tried to tell Jasmine that she thinks she's not good enough, she would vehemently disagree. She would tell you about how she exercises three times a week, eats organic, and volunteers with a group that helps at-risk teenage girls. She's doing all sorts of good things for herself, and she feels like that means she couldn't possibly be self-hating.

But Jasmine—whose dad is the service manager at a car

Catherine the Great

Okay, so I don't know if Kate Middleton is great or not, but when I think of girls who demonstrate self-love, I think she must have some. Why? Because of the way she handled her romance with Prince William. At first glance, it might seem that "Waity Katy," as the British tabloids dubbed her, is some kind of shrinking violet. I say, on the contrary! Only a girl with a lot of self-worth could have done things the way she did.

After all, even regular couples who date for many years can have arguments over when and whether the man will commit to marriage. In the case of Kate, a whole country was watching. I can imagine her writing herself a letter after a big fight with the prince over their future and putting it into her Intention Box:

> *Dear Kate,*
> *I know you are awesome whether or not this prince guy sees it, and you are worthy of being queen, whether or not he ever asks you to marry him. So just relax—you don't need him to prove to you that you are worthy. You already know you are. Which means you can wait as long as you need to, because if it's not him, it will be someone else.*
> *Love, Me*
> *(the future Catherine, Duchess of Cambridge)*

But in a way, the extended courtship was really more like an interminably long internship. Because when you think about it, in the paparazzi age, pretty much the *main* prerequisite for being the future queen of England—besides having a uterus that is open for business—is that you have your impulses under control. And girls who are unloving to themselves very rarely have their impulses under control. For ten long years, Kate had to sit tight and manage her own feelings—feelings around having to wait, not to mention having to watch millions of girls throw themselves at the prince's scepter. Kate had to keep it together. Which means she had to not impulsively have sex with someone else, show her tits while on spring break, upend a table in a restaurant out of anger, or tell William to go eff himself because, anyway, he is balding.

That could *not* have been easy. A girl who loves a guy more than she loves herself would have gone crackers waiting all that time. But Kate did it, and for her efforts, she is now a . . . duchess. Which is, I'm sure, not what she had in mind. To get what she wants, to be a princess or even queen, she is going to have to wait—maybe another ten years.

But Kate's proven she can do that.

dealership—can't stop going for the type of man I call the Quarterback. He's the guy with the Ivy League degree, the dad who's chief of surgery at a major hospital, the charity-circuit mom, and confidence bestowed upon him by a tony prep school and the body that comes from a lifetime of playing lacrosse. If this guy was a company, he'd be Apple, whereas Jasmine is a little more Applebee's. It's almost as if Jasmine is secretly trying to up her own stock price by merging with a company that's a whole lot fancier

and more valuable than hers. At least as far as the market is concerned.

Now, at first glance you might think Jasmine is shallow. But
there's something more going on here. Look a little closer and
you'll see that what attracts Jasmine to the Quarterback is that
she's coming from a place of *lack*—which is to say, deep down she
thinks she needs to make up for something. So she wants someone
who is "more" than what she is. (As she defines it.) If she didn't
believe this, she might discover she'd be happy with just a regular
guy with a regular family and a regular job.

Here's how you know for sure that Jasmine's situation is about
not being good enough: every time Jasmine is "rejected" (her
word) she uses that rejection to confirm to herself that there is
something so wrong with her that she will never find a great husband and be happy. She concludes, again, that she's just not
enough—pretty enough, smart enough, upscale enough—to get
the guy that she wants.

And in a sense, she is right. One quick look at real life con-
firms this. When I think about a quarterback, I think about Tom
Brady, the Super Bowl winner who plays for the New England
Patriots. And whom is he married to? Well, he dumped a gorgeous
Hollywood actress for an even more gorgeous supermodel. And
not just any supermodel—*the most famous supermodel in the
world.* He knows his company is Apple, and he's going for it.

It's basic biology that everyone is going to try to get with the
best possible mate. But when the whole I'm-not-good-enough
self-hate machine hijacks that process, you end up with a situation like Jasmine's. She spends all kinds of energy going for these
guys—who themselves are often going for similarly out-of-reach
girls—even though the clock is ticking and she's ready to settle
down now.

If you see yourself in Jasmine's situation, don't worry. What you're really dealing with here is just a *belief* that you are not enough, a belief that is completely fixable, *because it's not true.*

You just don't know it yet.

It's All Good

Your problem is always exactly what you need to cure your problem. Huh? Think of your problem like a push-up. No, not the bra. The worky-outy thing people in the army do to make themselves strong using only themselves and something that won't move, like a floor. In my metaphor, the problem—otherwise known as your false belief about you—is the floor. It is the immovable object. As you push against this immovable object you gain strength.

Pushing, in this example, is when you look at your false belief about you—that you are not enough—and instead of just caving in to it by lying there on the floor, you *counter* it by acknowledging to yourself that it is false. You push against it with the truth: *you are enough, right here and right now.*

Every time you do this, you are doing a push-up. And if you do this a lot—because you are choosing to be very disciplined about not letting false thoughts run around doing whatever they want in your mind—you will grow stronger. This is why you don't need to get rid of your false beliefs about you—you only have to challenge them. They contain exactly what you need to grow. This is also the reason people say, "It's all good." Even something bad is good—it offers the opportunity to grow.

In this way problem = strength.

Notes from My Life as a Cheated-on Wife

My third husband, Paul, left me. Wait, scratch that. Actually, I left him. But he cheated and made it impossible for me to stay. Infidelity is never easy to deal with, chiefly because it almost *always* challenges your sense of being good enough. For starters, as his cheating partner, my dear third husband chose a girl of twenty-one. (Thanks!) I was forty-one, so this, as you can imagine, gave me extra torque in my uphill climb to value myself. He also chose to start his new relationship after only nine months of marriage— or was it eight?—which really helped me feel like I make good choices in my life. And then there's my childhood background, with all the abandonment, my dad in prison—blah, blah, blah. You don't need to be a psychologist to see how much the self-hater in me wanted to conclude that *I just wasn't good enough and I never would be.*

Marrying Paul was like hitting a grand slam in the self-hate department. I would even go so far as to say that's *why* I chose him. Because on some intuitive level, I *knew* he was going to match up with my core belief that when you really love a man, he will leave you, or do something to make you leave him. Clearly, I had some major issues around self-worth, or I wouldn't have been attracted to Paul in the first place, because he was kind of a hot mess. (*So* cute, though!)

But life is super elegant in that it always tucks the solution to a problem right into the (possibly hidden) pocket of the problem itself. I learned this not in theory but because it was a Sunday afternoon and I was having to deal with the fact that a twenty-one-year-old was blowing up the cell phone of my seriously lame husband. By the end of the first day, I realized I only really had two choices: (1) give up on myself—and men—as hopeless, once and for all, and become bitter, or (2) decide that whatever I *thought* this meant about me, it was based on some old childhood idea and was therefore *false.* And ready to be healed.

I chose number two. Which was good news. Because it meant that sitting in front of me was not the massive wreckage of a marriage gone terribly awry and proof of how I am doomed forever in the area of relationships, but something much more hopeful: a giant, steaming pile of Learn How to Love Yourself Right Now.

Some Relevant Stuff About Men

Remember when I said this book is much more about you than it is about men? I really meant it. Because what that third husband helped me figure out—and what I hope you're beginning to understand—is that in order to move to the next level in the relationship game, a lady has to take 100 percent *total responsibility* for the men who are (or are not, as the case may be) in her life. One hundred percent.

That means you decide to acknowledge that it is *you* who brought these men into your life—even the bad ones. I'm not saying you consciously chose them. I'm not saying you wanted them to treat you badly. What I *am* saying is that nothing can change for you until you realize that at some level you have been *choosing* these men.

After all these years of getting married and dating, and a whole lot of failure (or "pre-success," as I like to call it), here's what I know: *men mirror back our deepest, most unconscious beliefs about ourselves.*

It's almost like every love relationship is a fairy tale where the man has been hypnotized by an evil fairy to do this reflecting-back-at-you thing. Not to hurt you—though it will feel like that until you wake up from your long, deep slumber—but *so that you can have a healing and know who you really are.*

Okay, maybe that's a little bit too Jungian (or maybe just a little too wacky), so let me try it another way. Think of a relationship with a guy as a movie depicting the way you relate to yourself, projected onto a large blank wall called Him. (Keep in mind he usually doesn't even know he is part of this movie experience.) In the movie, everything you think about yourself—from "I'm fat" to "I'm lovable" and whatever's in between—will be magically coming out of the Him character's mouth and reflected in Him's behavior. Where you are sure about you, the guy on the screen will be sure about you, and where you are not so sure, the guy on the screen will be buying you a gym membership for Valentine's Day. (True story.)

If you want to know what you deeply believe about yourself, just look at the behaviors and attitudes of the various Hims who've populated your life over the years. Do you see some patterns? Some common denominators from one guy to the next? Maybe you always find yourself dealing with a guy who is critical of you, or a guy who is controlling, or a guy who is unfaithful. It's tough to accept, but that's how you believe you should be treated.

When I first heard this idea, I scoffed, "Are you kidding me?" But you know you're dealing with a belief that's unconscious when it not only is preposterous but also *makes you mad.* Because no one gets angry about something unless deep down they know it's at least a little bit true.

Anyway, I encourage you to try on the idea for just a minute. You can always take it right back off if it doesn't fit. Because looking at men this way ultimately empowers you—now you see them, and your entire love life, in a whole new way. It's less about "Boy, was that guy a dick" and more about "OMFG, *that's* what I believe about myself?" You also get to see your progress. You know you are moving forward when you've upgraded the type of guy you attract from Furious Rager to Sometimes Sort of Angry but Still Reasonable About It.

Obviously, if you've got some unconscious beliefs about yourself that are not working for you, you're going to want to change those beliefs. But how?

How You're Going to Have to Change

You're going to have to *fire your ego*. If you think you're not good enough, you can be sure that your ego is the CEO of the corporation called You. This is just how the ego is, constantly comparing this thing to that thing and deciding one of them is better or worse. There are no equals in the world of the ego. It enjoys seeing nice people like you sweat. Think of the ego as the Wizard of Oz, back behind the curtain projecting itself up on a big screen, sounding super scary and intimidating. It spews hateful, mean things, all so that it can stay in charge.

Self-hate is not a natural state—we're not born hating ourselves. The idea that we are anything more or anything less than anyone else, or anywhere other than where we are supposed to be, is *always* generated by the ego. (This is true, BTW, for the man you're going to love as well. It's your ego that's going to try to tell you that he's better or worse than someone else, or better or worse than you.)

So what is the ego? First of all, it's not the *real* you, though it wants you to think that it is. The best way I know of to describe the ego is this: *the ego is the "you" who has the big voice and lives in your mind.*

If self-hate is the fourteen clowns that pile out of the car at the circus, the ego is the car itself. It is the part of yourself that drives you to do and say things that you will end up regretting, from sending that angry email to your sister because she "deserved" it to buying the BMW you can't possibly afford because you "deserved" it. Either way, the ego does not have your back.

Also? The ego talks. And talks and talks. It has a sharp tongue, like Simon Cowell on *American Idol* or Sue Sylvester on *Glee*. The ego snaps its fingers in a Z formation while wagging its head at you. It might sound smart, but it never has anything nice to say.

As long as your ego is running the show, you will be subject to its negative, self-hating messages about who you are. You will also be subject to mean messages about who other people are—people like the guys you're trying to date. In any case, if you believe these messages, much of the time *you will not be able to be a kind, loving person.* Not to yourself, or to anyone else. Obviously, this is going to have a serious effect on your relationships.

The bottom line is that you can only love a man as well as you love yourself. Your ability to be compassionate and kind to someone—even when that someone has just done something really stupid, and even when that someone is you—comes from your ability to be compassionate and kind to yourself. That's why it is said that kindness is *extended*—because you give it from the pile of kindness you already have. And if you only have a little pile, you're going to find marriage tough going.

So how do you get a bigger pile?

Spiritual Stuff That Will Help You Change

You've got to get you some *self-love.* If you've ever read a self-help book or watched *Oprah,* you're probably so sick of hearing about how spiritual it is to practice self-love—maybe to the point that you think it's become a horrible cliché. It kind of has. But that doesn't change the fact that your ability to love yourself has everything to do with your ability to be in a relationship, as well as—and this is the whole reason we're talking about it here—your ability to change the things that are standing in the way of your getting into a relationship.

If you're like I was, you may not even be really sure what it means. For one thing, the term "self-love" is often used interchangeably with "self-esteem," but they're not the same thing. Self-esteem is thinking your ass looks especially cute in those jeans. Self-love is when you're kind to yourself even when it doesn't.

If I had to break it down in the simplest way possible, I'd say that *self-love is when you treat yourself the way a very good parent or grandma-type person would treat you.*

So what does that look like? It doesn't mean you indulge yourself—like buying yourself a new Fendi bag when you had a bad day at work. It means you are more *loving,* more nurturing, and more supportive . . . of yourself. This is how the parents you *wish* you'd had would have treated you: you set firm boundaries for yourself, you expect a lot of yourself, and you hold yourself to high (but not abusively high) expectations, because you want yourself to have an awesome life.

When something bad happens, you take responsibility for it—you don't blame yourself or others. Especially when things go wrong (and this is life, so things are *going* to go wrong), you treat yourself the way someone would lovingly treat their child—you don't say anything mean to you, you don't tell yourself you're stupid, or that you deserved it, or that something is wrong with you.

You don't say anything to yourself that you can't see Betty White saying to you.

A Set of Tracks

Your relationship with yourself is like a set of tracks that leads men to you. Wherever those tracks lead within—whether it is to a place of self-love or to a place of fear—the men carrying those qualities are the men who will reach you.

Fine, so we're clear on that. But let's go back to what I was saying about self-love being the most important ingredient in change. Here's why: in order for change to happen, you have to *allow yourself to know* that change needs to happen. But in years of talking to women who are going through this process of learning to love themselves and learning how to make changes, I've noticed something. Allowing this knowledge to percolate to the surface of your mind can only happen if you know another, very important thing deep down: *that you will still love yourself if you admit that you need to change.*

Let me explain this a little more. It used to be that I couldn't even hear what I was doing wrong in a relationship because whatever it was, it could only mean one thing: I was totally unlovable! First and foremost, by me.

For instance, a boyfriend once said to me that I talked too much and he felt he could never get a word in edgewise. This is a pretty simple criticism, and it was probably also very true, but still, *I could hardly hear it.* The reason I couldn't hear it is because there was no way I could love myself as a person who talks too much. I would argue *to the death* to convince him that it's not that I talk too much but that he doesn't talk enough and it's really all his problem. Obviously. And if I had to throw in some observations about his dysfunctional family upbringing to bolster my point, then oh well—it's not like I was wrong. Which leads to the other big complaint boyfriends have had about me: how I think I'm right all the time. Those are just the two biggies at the top of a long list of stuff I do and/or used to do.

Unfortunately, as long as I can't receive the criticism—because I won't be able to consider myself lovable if I allow it to be true— I can't change.

You might be wondering what it actually *looks like* to love yourself. Well, here's how it looked for me. Every time I had a thought where I told myself how stupid I was to have married Paul, I simply said, calmly and quietly: "I love you, Tracy." Then when I could hear my self (really, it was my ego) telling me I was old and washed up because I'd been tossed overboard in favor of a twenty-one-year-old, I would say it again: "I love you, Tracy." And when I realized that I was going to have to rebuild my life from the ground up at forty-one, I just said it again: "I love you, Tracy." I said it every time I had a negative thought or feeling about myself.

I said it a lot.

And I tried to mean it. At first it felt weird, but gradually the words began to feel less hollow. I started to experience the feeling behind the words—*I love you*—and it felt good. It meant I was standing behind me, I could comfort me, I had compassion for me, and I could reassure me that everything was going to be okay.

It worked, and not just to get me through the immediate aftermath of the breakup. Going forward, I know that no matter what happens in a relationship with a guy, *I will be okay.* And that, as it turns out, was the thing that had been missing from my relationships all along.

What Your Grandma Knows That She Would Kindly Like to Tell You

So let's recap Chapter 7:

- ***You hate yourself.*** You think you're not good enough, and it's getting in the way of letting someone into your life. *It's not true!* You're wonderful, even when you're totally imperfect.
- ***Men are like mirrors.*** They show you your deepest beliefs about yourself. Look for the patterns—where do you need to work on your self-worth?
- ***Fire your ego.*** The ego is the big voice in your head that thinks it is Simon Cowell. Tell it the show's over and it's time to go home. If you believe what it tells you, you will have a very hard time being a nice person. Especially to a man.
- ***Learn to love yourself.*** Your ability to treat yourself like a very loving person would treat you is crucial to your ability to be in a healthy relationship. Because you can only love someone else as much as you love yourself.

8. You're a Liar

Or, Deluding Yourself and Other Tragedies

1. Have you told someone you don't want a relationship when you really do?
2. Have you ignored all the warning signs about a guy because you wanted him?
3. Have you hidden details of a relationship because your friends would tell you to end it if they knew?

MAYBE IT STARTS LIKE THIS: you meet a guy you're attracted to. That almost *never* happens, so even before your first conversation with him is over, you're already kind of secretly hoping—way, way in the back of your mind—that this could work. Another part of you is already sure it won't, since you've been through this a zillion times, and if things had ever worked out, you wouldn't be sitting here right now, sipping a mojito and wondering whether you're going to like living in the neighborhood this guy just told you he lives in. He also said something that made it clear he's not really available for a serious relationship, but you're tired of stopping things before they even start, so you give him a chance anyway. People change their minds all the time. Plus he's effing *cute*.

Over the next couple of weeks, things progress from making out to, well, hooking up. It's not dating exactly, but close enough. You go to dinner, movies, and art openings, but you each pay for yourselves and you invite him as often as he invites you. Still, you enjoy his company and there's a possibility it could turn into something more. Isn't there? Of course there is. People change their minds all the time.

Though you would never admit it, you know (way, way in the back of your mind) that if you tell him what you really want—marriage, a baby, a home—he will leave. Probably later this afternoon. So you just tell him how perfect this arrangement is because you only want to hang out and have sex for fun! You love having fun sex! And you don't want to get in a relationship at all! You swear! You just love hanging with him!

In other words: *you lie.* And you have no idea how it's affecting your love life.

What It's Really About

There are a thousand ways to lie in a relationship, but only one of them really matters: when you *lie to yourself.* Self-deception is probably the most destructive thing you can do to your prospects for a happy, healthy relationship. Why? Because it's the thing that makes all the stuff in chapters 1 through 7 possible. It's the muscle—the enforcer, really—behind all the other behaviors that are keeping you single. If you weren't deluding yourself, you would be forced to reckon with the way the casual sex, anger, fear, perfectionism, craziness, and all the rest of it are affecting your relationships—or lack of them. And not reckoning with it is keeping you stuck.

Lying is almost always motivated by one thing: getting what
you want. If you really examine your deceptive behavior, you'll
see that you wanted someone or something and you couldn't have
it—at least not with a clear conscience—unless you lied to them
or to yourself. So you did what you thought you had to do, and then
your psyche helpfully erased all traces of your crime—so that you
would never catch yourself. This process is so common there's
even a special word for it: "denial."

It's crucial to your future marriage that you deal with the ways
in which you lie to yourself. A strong relationship requires two
people who are authentic—with themselves, and with each other.
An authentic guy will "smell" your lies and steer clear. Even if
you do manage to sneak a lie past a guy you want, if he doesn't
notice your deception, you can be sure there is some way in which
he is putting one over on himself. Or on you. Neither of which is
particularly awesome.

So let's talk about some common situations where you might lie
to yourself about a man. As you will see, there's a staggering
amount of variety—not.

- **He's inappropriate.** He's married. He's nineteen. He's got a
  major poker problem. Whatever it is, a less delusional woman
  would immediately reject him. But not you. You think you're
  going to hang in there until the problem is solved—most likely
  by you.
- **He's not happening.** He's married. He's nineteen. He's got a
  needle dangling out of his arm. Whatever it is, he doesn't want
  you—or at least, not badly enough to solve the problem that
  you are begging him to let you solve.
- **He's unavailable.** He's married. He's nineteen. He watches
  porn three hours a day. Whatever it is, he's busy. Leave him

alone. He keeps asking you to, but you won't listen. You think he's just "scared" to get close to you because he's got problems and needs your help.

Then there is my favorite lie of all:

- ■ ***He's just a friend.*** You know him from work, or from around town, or maybe even the two of you used to be in a relationship. Whatever it is, you're thinking, *Well, at least he doesn't watch three hours of porn a day.* News flash: friends are when you *don't* want to have sex with someone. If you want to have sex with someone—even if it's not that much—you aren't just friends. You're friends who want to have sex but it just hasn't happened (yet). Which means all you are doing now is having friendly coffee dates and possibly even working on a friendly "project" together until the time comes where you can slip and fall on his penis. If you can't acknowledge this, you're being immature and it's no wonder you're not married.

If you're trying to get with any of the above types of guy, chances are you're keeping a lot of the details about him to yourself. Lying requires this. Not that you don't talk about him to anyone who will listen—your therapist, your waxer, your fourteen thousand closest friends. You just conveniently leave out the shocking parts of the story. Instead of being married, he's separated (while living in the same house and sleeping in the same bed with his wife). Instead of being nineteen, he's really immature (which is normal for someone who's nineteen). Instead of having a needle hanging out of his arm, he's edgy (as if edgy is really all that great). You blunt the bad thing to the point where it almost sounds good. And you're so persuasive, even *you* start to believe it.

The Second Biggest Delusion

If "we're just friends" is the biggest delusion, the second biggest delusion is "he'll change." I will never forget what a long-married acquaintance (okay, hairdresser) said about six months into my third, disastrous marriage. She'd been married twelve years and her number-one piece of advice was chillingly simple: *if he never changed a single thing about himself, could you live with him exactly as he is right now?*

Her question sent a shiver down my spine. Because the answer for me was no . . . or at least not without anti-anxiety medication. I was dealing with a guy who, if he was a car, was totaled. Like when a lady hit my parked 1984 Volvo station wagon. It didn't matter that the car was amazing—the fact that there were major dents in two doors and the front quarter panel made the cost of repairing it way more than the $2,600 the car was worth. What my hairdresser was talking about is when you have a really decent Honda that only needs the dude equivalent of a new set of seat covers. Or even if he needs a new bumper—well, you can live without that. But if you're having to replace the, say, *engine*? Maybe not.

It's not that guys never change. They do, sometimes. But only if they feel like it. Going deeper into a relationship—i.e., moving in, getting engaged, or marrying—while gambling that a guy is going to change something basic to his personality or important to your (or his) value system is crazy. You have to assume that the guy standing in front of you is going to stay exactly the way he is.

This is probably a good thing for you, too. Allowing a man to simply be the way he is right now—until he decides to grow or change, *if* he ever decides to grow and change—is called loving someone unconditionally. This is what everyone wants! Including you. And if you want to get it, you're going to have to give it.

But not really. Underneath your spin you know there's something wrong here. You know how I know? Because you're lying about it.

Notes from My Life as a Woman Who Ignored at Her Peril What She Knew

I've had this experience firsthand. Take my third husband, for example. I knew from the very beginning that there was no way the relationship was going to work, but I pretended I didn't. I just didn't want to know! I tucked the truth deep into a little spot just outside of my peripheral vision. But even if I could have admitted it, it wouldn't have mattered. Because I wanted that man! Paul was cool and handsome, and he had a great job and an apartment you couldn't help but imagine yourself living in. We dated for three very intense days before I told him if I slept with him I would get attached to him and was he someone who wanted to be attached to? I needed to know if he was available for a relationship. I was even proud of myself for being so up-front.

It worked—but not the way I wanted it to. Paul promptly disappeared. After being in almost constant contact for all three days (of our very intense relationship), he simply vanished. I was bummed in the worst way. The way where it's not even justified because you hardly even knew the guy—yet somehow he got into your world and fucked it all up. I did do one thing different, though: for maybe the first time ever, I simply let him go. I didn't call, I didn't write, I didn't "accidentally" run into him. I didn't chase him in any way.

This was sort of a miracle, because my usual dating pattern—when I wasn't married—was to be either (1) pining after someone or (2) chasing after someone. I acted as if love meant trying to finagle a guy into figuring out that I'm awesome. But at thirty-nine, I was beginning to understand some of the mistakes I had been making with men, the chasing thing chief among them. Paul had made it clear that, for the time being, he wasn't interested, and I practiced letting him go. Yay, me! I felt like I was really growing up, and in many ways I was.

So imagine my delight when, five weeks later, my new technique proved effective beyond my dreams—Paul called me! He said he had been thinking about me, and asked if we might try again. Naturally, I was thrilled.

But underneath my excitement I had a quiet but very insistent feeling in the pit of my stomach that went like this: *This is major trouble. This relationship is not going to work. This guy does not know what he is doing and he is going to drag me down with him.* Still, sometimes learning is a sort of two-steps-forward-one-step-back thing. Unwilling to let Paul go again, I ventured forth, against my inner knowing, my inner truth.

Technically, I <u>listened</u> to the feeling; I just didn't do anything about it. I simply let it be there as I dated, moved in with, then married Paul—all within ten months. And nine months after that, I caught him cheating. *Ugh.*

There's a lot more to this story, obviously, but I can take full responsibility for my part in what happened by going back to that moment where I knew the truth and then just as quickly un-knew it. Paul wasn't a great guy in many ways, but if I had been able to be honest with myself, his not being a great guy wouldn't have had any effect on me at all. I'm the one who opened the door to his BS—when I lied to myself.

Taking responsibility for it means I never have to do it again! Because in my experience, super-bad shit does not just happen. It happens with plenty of warning signs.

Warning signs that I was lying to myself about.

Why Claire's Not Married

A girl I used to exercise with has another version of this going on. At thirty-eight, Claire had been dating Jason for a few months when "they" finally decided it would just "make more sense" to move in together. The thing is, moving in together wasn't Jason's idea, and he wasn't proposing marriage. Though neither one of them ever said it explicitly, the whole project was Claire's.

Not surprisingly, one year after they settled in the bigger, better apartment—the one that represented a committed life together—Jason moved out. He simply wasn't ready to make that kind of commitment yet—it just took him a year to admit it to himself. But Jason, a record producer, didn't just leave—he decided to have an affair with a young singer-songwriter on his way out. This scorched-earth exit would ensure that Claire had no choice but to get honest about Jason's unwillingness to marry her.

More than a year later, Claire is still furious with him. She feels Jason deceived her, and—though he is definitely 50 percent responsible for what happened—he was only able to do so because Claire was deceiving herself.

If she were to look a little closer, Claire would see that her desire to make such a big move with Jason was *precisely because* she knew Jason wasn't committed, and she wanted to move things along. She was hoping the new beginning was going to *bring about* the commitment, instead of being *the result* of it. She got things turned around.

And as long as she can't admit to herself that she knew all along that Jason wasn't committed, Claire can continue to play the victim and blame Jason for being the bad guy. In reality, Jason was the person in the relationship who simply said out loud what both of them already knew. He didn't handle it well by having an affair. But the affair didn't change Claire's underlying problem—that Jason wasn't choosing her as a wife, and that she allowed herself to go into denial over it.

Again, we have to go back to the principle we talked about in Chapter 2: *we are always finding our match out there.* Claire and Jason were both deceptive—Jason was deceiving Claire, and Claire was deceiving herself. The truth was right there—but Claire was unwilling to hear it. And being unwilling to hear the truth is just the flip side of being unwilling to tell it.

No Second Date

I had this one relationship where the guy came over to my house to watch a movie on the VCR (this was a long time ago) and essentially *never left.* We didn't have a second date because our first date basically never ended! After a couple of months we realized we were living together. Yes, he had an apartment with a roommate, but he didn't use it. After a year, we finally made it official and moved in together—by filling out a change of address form at the post office.

You won't be surprised to learn that the relationship did not end well. It was over when I realized that, in my mind at least, I was engaged to him—but he was still dating me. Because as far as he was concerned, I wasn't the one. Surprise! He didn't come right out and say this, but over time it became really obvious. Of course, I was pretty angry about it.

Eventually, though, I had to look at how that happened. And that was no mystery. After all, *we never even went on a second date.* That's how. By "moving in" together on our first date, I never had to deal with my uncertainty about the relationship. It was simply on and we were simply in it.

I've always had a hard time with the beginning stages of a relationship because that's where I have the most anxiety about whether or not the relationship is going to last. I'm always super eager to jump into phase two or phase three— where you know you're going to be together forever. It's a big part of why I've always wanted to get married. I (somewhat childishly) thought that if we declared our commitment for life, it would be thus.

Moving in together on day one was my next best plan. But while I might have been attempting to do away with my uncertainty, all I actually did was defer it until three years later, when push came to shove and my boyfriend and I faced a situation that—in order to get through it together— would require a genuine commitment. Which I then found out I did not have.

Discovering this was a painful lesson, but once I tracked down exactly how it happened, it is one I will never have to learn again.

Unfortunately, Claire's ongoing anger at Jason suggests that she hasn't figured out her part yet—that she was lying to herself. And until she does, she's not ready for marriage.

Some Relevant Stuff About Men

So let's talk for a minute about how men operate. In my experience, most guys will not lie to you. At least not directly. They might skirt around certain topics, but they won't come out and say yes if they mean no when you ask them point-blank if they're interested in getting married anytime soon.

What they will do is let you lie to yourself. Let's say you're super convincing when you say you could be interested in a friends-with-benefits type of arrangement. A guy might deceive himself into thinking you know what you're talking about—even though friends with benefits hasn't worked for the last three women he tried it with. (At least not past the first month.) But eventually this type of situation just gets too cumbersome (or painful) for most guys, and they learn to detect whether a woman is *really* capable of friends with benefits, or if she's secretly trying to do more of a thing where she acts like a temp worker hoping to get hired full-time if she really wows on the job.

Then there is a more pernicious sort of lying men sometimes do, the kind Jason was engaged in—where they take all the actions of being committed, without necessarily being committed. They move in with you, they talk about the future, they may even go halves on a major piece of furniture—but in their hearts they are still only dating you. I have a guy friend who calls this "deep dating." It's where a guy takes his sweet time trying on an idea of you, and of life with you. When trying to explain it to me, my friend diagrammed it like this:

1
10
100
1,000
10,000

Each of these numbers represents a point in the relationship—how many times you've had sex with him. (What can I say? Sometimes this is how guys think.) At each spot, the man has a different idea of what the relationship is, and what it could be. At numbers 1, 10, and 100, he simply does not yet (at least in his mind) have enough information about you to make a lifetime commitment. Even if you've already let him move into your apartment. (Like I said, you probably shouldn't have done that.)

But we live in a culture of so-called compulsory monogamy—which is to say that if you're a woman like me, you are *not* going to have sex more than a hundred times with a guy who is not in a "committed" relationship with you. This fact leaves a man in a tough position—either he's going to go along with your monogamy program while he makes up his mind about the long-term prospects of the relationship, or he's going to tell you the truth (that he's still thinking it over, ten months later) and watch you bail for a guy who *will* go along with it.

According to my friend—who is a biologist, mind you—this leads men and women into a sort of marriage-and-dating arms race, where the man matches the interballistic continental missile of your refusal to have sex with him a hundred times outside of a committed relationship with his own Star Wars–type defense shield: deep dating.

I share this idea with you not because I like it but because I think it happens a lot. It's the reason that a thirty-three or thirty-six or thirty-nine-year-old woman sometimes finds herself breaking up with a guy she's been living with (possibly for years) because she thought she was going to marry him, but he, it turns out, was only dating her.

Deep dating her.

There are really only two things you can do to defend yourself against this. One, *do not move in with a guy without marrying him unless you don't care if you never marry him.* Like I always say: a man rarely changes while you're fucking him and cooking him dinner.

And two, you're going to have to *get honest.* With yourself, and with men.

How You're Going to Have to Change

Getting honest is easier said than done. First you have to learn how to know when you're lying. There's something about the human psyche that is extremely talented at not knowing what it doesn't want to know. Our brains evolved over eleventy-billion years or so to make sure that all you really care about is harvesting some particularly hardy sperm. And if you have to lie to yourself to get it, fine. Nature couldn't give a fuck.

But modern life is considerably more complicated than that. Because we live longer, the marriages we make last a lot longer than those of our Neanderthal forebears, and in order to be happy in them, we have to choose wisely. Having a successful marriage now means more than just having babies and hunting lions. It's about knowing who we are, knowing who we are partnering with, and making sure (to the best of your ability—no one has a crystal ball) that it's a match.

I can always tell when a woman is lying to herself about a rela-

tionship. In her conversation, she will make statements that rationalize, minimize, justify, and deny what a guy is saying or doing,
or *not* saying and not doing. She tells me he doesn't drink *that*
much, or that she's only seeing him because his marriage has
been over for *years,* or that she's sure he loves her even though
nothing in his behavior demonstrates that love. When you hear
yourself making excuses in this way, wave a red flag in front of
your own face. Because you can be very sure that without some
kind of intervention, the relationship is going to run into trouble,
and the person who is going to have to deal with the aftermath is
you.

Another sign it might be time to sit yourself down and get honest: when you're having completely different conversations with
your girlfriends than you are having with your man. If you're saying things about your boyfriend to your girlfriends that you would
never say to his face—major doubts, major criticisms—pay attention. While it's probably wise to be mindful of not harming another person unnecessarily, if you are telling your girlfriends
deal-breaking things about your relationship that you are keeping
from the guy you are seeing, you are lying.

At their worst, lies withhold from the other person information
they need to make better decisions about what is best for them.
An obvious example: I don't tell you I have herpes. A less obvious
example: I don't tell you that what I really want is a guy who's also
a Lutheran. The most common example of all: I'm looking for a
long-term relationship and I don't care if you aren't; I'm going to
date you anyway. There's a level of integrity required in a good
marriage, and if you're doing any of these, you don't have it.

Another way we lie to ourselves—one that seriously damages
our marriage prospects—is by hanging on to a guy we know we
can't, won't, or don't want to marry. I once spent *years* dating a

man who, if I got really honest, I knew wasn't the one (or in my case, the fourth). The truth was, I *knew* he wasn't right for me, but I wasn't ready to let go of him just yet.

This happens a lot. Not surprisingly, not wanting to let go is the number one reason people hang on. (Of course it is.) Again, it comes back to fear—fear you'll never find someone else or fear you'll look back and regret letting go of the one guy you *did* have. Even if you're not sure you really want a particular man, you don't want to lose your option on him, either. It gets confusing, too, because sometimes you're not sure whether you're supposed to settle down (or just settle) for the guy in front of you, or if you're supposed to hold out for something else. That can be a very difficult question to answer, admittedly. But if you are really honest with yourself, you can be sure that you will know when you know.

The other thing you might be hoping is that eventually he'll wake up and figure out that you're the one. I'm sorry to say I've got news for you: he's never going to figure that out, because he already knows you're not. You know it, too, or you wouldn't have to lie to yourself about him.

I spend a lot of time talking to men about what moves them from dating to commitment to marriage. The vast majority of them say that they know pretty close to immediately whether they would be willing to consider a woman for a long-term relationship. If they are, they start pursuing that relationship. If they aren't, they do little—maybe some halfhearted calling or texting in the hopes of some casual sex—or they do nothing.

By now you might be asking what you should do when you realize you're lying to yourself about a guy. There is only one thing to do: walk away. Not that it's going to be easy. There is nothing in the dating world—and I mean nothing—more difficult than walking away from a guy you really like. Especially if you've had one or two or five or six good times with him. Triple especially if you had multiple orgasms. Lots of gals would play a pretty good game of Twister—right foot red, left foot green, right hand yellow—in order to come up with a way to keep enjoying that guy. There must be a way to manage the part of the relationship that's unmanageable! Maybe if you just saw him on weekends, or even once a month . . . ? It's hard to let go.

But let go you must if you want to move forward. Part of you will hope it's only temporary—and sometimes it turns out to be. I see this most often when a guy doesn't want to commit, change, or develop in some important way, but he knows he really loves you. The key here is that *he* knows he loves you—not *you* know he loves you. If this is your situation, leave him. But let him go completely—no calling, texting, emails, or, God forbid, booty calls. If he's going to wake up to his love for you, it will happen in a month or two.

If it goes much beyond that, you can figure he's not coming back. Then you can have a good cry, keep yourself super busy for a while, and maybe do a girls' weekend in Santa Barbara. It won't be fun, but the good news is that—because you've been disciplined by not calling, texting, emailing, or, God forbid, booty-calling—by that time you will be well on your way to getting over him.

What you *can't* do is fake out the universe. If you're pretending to yourself that you're totally over him but you're still really holding a space for him, you won't move forward. So make sure you practice your self-honesty, because you're committed to yourself and you are worth it.

Spiritual Stuff That Will Help You Change

The key is to *know yourself.* Emerging from self-deception is about getting into a process of understanding who you are and what you need—in a man, and in life. If you know who you are, you are much less likely—less *able,* really—to fool yourself into doing things you know aren't right or good for you. You just have to wake up to yourself. And in order to do that, you have to *excavate.*

The process of discovering more of the truth about you is like an archeological dig. You start by looking for areas where you are unconscious. One way to know where you have stuff buried is to look at things people say about you that, as I said earlier, not only are preposterous but *also make you mad.* Like the stuff in this book. Whatever makes your heart go a little faster, whatever makes you want to write me an impassioned or defensive or angry email about how wrong I am—those are the broken vase handles sticking up out of the ground. Start digging.

Next, check out what kinds of things in relationships spark emotional reactions that seem bigger than they should be. Is it when you think someone is lying to you? When someone is condescending? When someone is withholding? There is a saying: "If I'm hysterical, it's historical." You will need to make some of this stuff conscious if you are going to stop lying to yourself, since lying to yourself is just your mind's way of keeping painful truths or painful realizations out of your awareness.

Be prepared to involve yourself in this process for a long time—probably the rest of your life. Because when you start carefully brushing away all the dirt around those broken vase handles, you will quickly realize *there's a whole fucking city down there*!

(Yeah, it's called being human.) Gingerly excavating your ancient artifacts is the work of life. And really, what else do you have to do that's more important than that? Go to the movies? The truth shall set you free.

But you have to want to know. This is the final piece of the lying puzzle. It is crucial to begin to let into your mind things your fear is trying to keep out. It's not hard to understand why your subconscious places painful things safely out of view—the truth hurts. Still, as painful as it may be, the truth only hurts for a minute in lifetime terms. Lying hurts *forever*, because it keeps you perpetually stuck in life situations that aren't working.

So how do you begin? Here's one way. While you are doing something mindless, like driving, doing the dishes, knitting, or walking, try asking yourself this question: "What am I not seeing?"

Then look away from the question. Go back to your mindless activity. As you continue gardening, folding clothes, washing the car, or whatever it is that you're doing, you may begin to notice a sort of answer bubbling up to the surface. Sometimes it comes as an image, a phrase, or a word. Don't worry if at first you don't recognize anything. If you regularly ask questions like "What do I need to know to move forward in my life?" you will absolutely enter into a dialogue with the part of your mind that is the container for stuff you know but which you don't think you're ready to know. That part of your mind is just waiting for you to be in agreement with knowing more. However, since we have free will (or seem to, anyway), we need to *ask*. It sounds strange, but it works.

Once you get the hang of that, you can take this exercise to the next level. Before you go to sleep, ask yourself for a dream that answers a question you've been wanting to know the answer to:

"Is John Doe the guy for me? Am I in denial about John Doe?" Do this until you start to get some clarity. It won't take long. The mind has a way of revealing what you need to know the moment you are willing to know it.

Another good way to dialogue with your unconscious mind is especially useful for times you feel a vague sense of unease or discomfort but you're not exactly sure what it is. Take a half hour to lie down in your bed, pull up your covers, and ask your mind what it's trying to tell you. Just say to yourself: "What is going on? What is happening here?" Then lie there quietly while you see what surfaces. Pay attention to the thoughts that come into your mind. It may be a bit like reading a dream, but if you do this regularly, you will be surprised at how much information you will gain access to about your relationships and your life.

What Your Former BFF Wanted to Tell You but Never Did

Now to recap Chapter 8:

- **You're a liar.** You're dishonest with men and, more important, with yourself, and it's keeping you from seeing the consequences of your behavior.
- **Be real.** Telling a guy you are willing to be friends with benefits when you really want a relationship is lying. Besides, it's undignified—the relationship equivalent of asking to volunteer at a company that didn't want to hire you.
- **Check yourself.** If you hear yourself rationalize, minimize, justify, or deny a guy's behavior, you can be sure something's going on. That's where self-deception starts. It doesn't mean

you have to leave the guy. But it does mean you need to wake up.

- **_Excavate._** It's the best way to avoid self-deception. Actively get into a dialogue with the part of your mind that always knows the truth. Be willing to find out what is below the level of your conscious awareness.

9. You're a Dude
Or, How to Get into Your Feminine and Realize You Are a Prize

1. Does it sometimes feel like if it weren't for sex, you would have no real need for a man?
2. When you meet a guy that you like, do you tend to chase after him or try to make it easy for him to date you?
3. Do you sometimes jump into sex as a way to feel more in control of a new relationship?

CAN WE JUST TALK ABOUT BEYONCÉ for a minute? Not about the fact that she's gorgeous, talented, powerful, and rich. (So rich!) Nor that she's married to a super-famous guy she's just had a baby with. (Jay-Z, and a baby girl named Blue Ivy, in case you've never heard of *Us Weekly.*) Or that she's got it going on to the point that I wouldn't be surprised if by now she and her mom have figured out a way to grow her hair blond in addition to everything they're doing with that fashion line. That's all interesting, but it's not why I'm devoting a whole paragraph to a pop star in my funny, self-helpy, big-sistery, spiritual-like, no-nonsense book about why you're not married.

The reason I'm doing that is because Beyoncé is like a singing, dancing Christiane Amanpour—a correspondent reporting from the man/woman front lines. Her biggest hits—"Independent Women," "Run the World (Girls)," and of course the ubiquitous "Single Ladies (Put a Ring on It)"—sum up something so basic, so far-reaching, so important, and so *fixable* about what's going on with American women that I want to spend a whole chapter on it.

It's something that—if none of this other stuff quite fits and you are beginning to suspect there is some intangible thing about you that is keeping the love away, but you have no idea what it is— I can be 97 percent sure is at least part of the underlying cause, and probably a big part. And that something is: *you act like a dude.*

Listen closer to those Beyoncé songs—the women in them are utterly self-reliant. They make money, they buy their own stuff, they have sex with men, and when they're done, they tell the men to go home. Not that this is a bad thing, and not like we all have to time-travel back to the place where women had to depend on men for everything, but is anyone really surprised that the fellow in the "Single Ladies" song didn't put a ring on it? A better question might be, why should he? You don't need him for anything! Everyone knows guys like to *do* shit, not just hang around watching you do it.

In fact, this whole acting-like-a-dude situation brings me to one of the big secrets of the world of mating, and one of the reasons I know I can say with certainty that you are way closer to finding your perfectly imperfect partner than you may think. You don't have to be billboard-gorgeous to find a great husband. You can be just a regular girl from Cincinnati, but if you have this one thing, this thing I'm about to spend a whole chapter talking about, you will find that men are going to be attracted to you in a way they never have been before.

And the good news is *you already have it.* All women have it. You were born with it. You just need to let it . . . happen.

What It's Really About

I'm talking about your *inner feminine*. Some people call it "feminine energy," "the feminine principle," the "sacred feminine," or maybe even something ridiculous like "wild woman self," but the meaning is basically the same—it's about being rooted in the *feminine aspect of life*. It's so important that from here on out I am going to call it the Feminine, with a capital *F.*

So what is the Feminine? Well, it's not (necessarily) about ruffles, high heels, or unicorns and rainbows. The Feminine I am talking about is something both men and women have, just like they both have a Masculine. And like the earth has a north pole and a south pole—opposites attract.

The Chinese actually came up with a symbol to illustrate this Masculine/Feminine polarity—the yin/yang. You've seen it before, probably in a bookstore next to the crystals, or as a tattoo on a girl who smells like patchouli. It looks like this:

Yin = Feminine. Yang = Masculine. In Eastern philosophy, these two "things" (I'm using that word loosely) aren't separate or opposite but interrelated, *part of a whole*—swimming together, chasing each other, inseparable. They are *energies* that are seemingly opposite but are really connected, like the two sides of a seesaw. Intimate relationships always contain an interplay between these two forces, the Masculine and the Feminine. Both people in a relationship cannot play the same role at the same time, any more than both people in ballroom dancing can be the one dancing backward, or both people can be driving a car at the same time. And it's not even about sexual orientation. It's as true of same-sex couples (like where one person is the butch and one is the femme) as it is of male-female couples.

You probably already know intuitively what these two energies are like, but I want to give you a little more about how they work. The Masculine conquers things. It *thinks* about stuff (as opposed to *feeling* it), argues, builds bridges and skyscrapers, keeps score, makes money, goes to the moon, and plays to *win*. It's hard and dry. It wants to be empty: in a man cave, or watching the game, or sitting side by side with other dudes and not really saying much of anything. Most of all, it wants to be free.

The Feminine is why you're reading this book. It's about relationship, connection, the impulse to love and to nurture. The Feminine wants to create a home, tend a garden, raise a family, hang curtains, and deeply intuit the people around her. It wants to be in community—especially with other women—and build society by setting boundaries for the Masculine, which, without the presence of the Feminine, can tend to see people and things (like the planet) as resources to be exploited instead of resources to be nurtured. The Feminine is soft, wild, unpredictable, and beautiful—like nature. More than anything, the Feminine wants to love. When it comes to relationships, these two energies attract each other. And they also unleash each other's power.

The deal is this: if you're a regular American chick who goes to work every day and focuses on performing tasks and accomplishing them in a directed, linear, focused way, you are spending the majority of your waking hours in your Masculine. And if you're spending the majority of your waking hours in your Masculine without doing anything to build your Feminine, you might find yourself in your thirties with more to offer a man than ever before—but with seemingly less ability to attract him. And it's not because you're getting older. It's because you're overdeveloped in the Masculine side of yourself.

You see this a lot with career ladies. (I say this as a career lady.) The same qualities it takes to develop an awesome professional life are the exact same qualities that will mess up your love life but good. This *does not* mean I think women should quit their jobs and join a quilting circle. That's too simplistic. What it means is that your Feminine is a gift, and it is the gift that *you*—the woman in your relationship—have signed up to bring (like you might bring a casserole to a potluck), most likely without even knowing it. A man *could* bring it; it's just that, generally speaking, he won't. Nor does he want to.

In my mind, trying to conduct a relationship from your Masculine is like a right-handed person writing with their left hand—you can do it, but it's not where you flow. The Masculine is not the center of your power as a woman.

So how do you move into your Feminine? Well, at first, practicing the Feminine principle in a partnership will look like Opposite Day. You're going to stop doing some stuff that comes so naturally you probably don't even know you're doing it. And then you're going to start doing some stuff that will really bug you at first. Here are some examples of what you're going to want to do:

1. *Be willing to need him.* Earlier I jokingly said men like to do stuff—and that's true. But that desire to *do* really comes out of

a deeper need: to be useful to you. And if you can't need a man, he can't be useful to you. When I say need, I don't mean that you're *needy*. I mean you let him serve you. You let him matter to you. You allow him to take a deep place in your heart—and your body—to the degree that if he were to leave, you would hurt. If he can't hurt you, you're still too defended.

2. *Stop arguing.* If you're like me, this is really hard. If you're talking to a man and you're trying to be right, you are in your Masculine energy. This is fine if you are at work, but presumably you're not trying to have sex with anyone at work. With your man, you have a different objective—to love. And simply put, arguing doesn't create love. Arguing is, by definition, focused on differences. Sometimes a good argument can be stimulating to the relationship, but only as long as you can keep the *love* in the conversation bigger than the fight, or your need to be right.

3. *Open up.* Another requirement for a loving relationship is openness. Being open is challenging. Our lives are busy and stressful and there are a million little things each day that can make you want to close up: commuting, taxes, and the asshole in Sales, to name a few. If you want to attract more love into your life, practice being open. Just imagine your heart has a pink light shining out of it. Turn the light up, and *lead with it.* Just beam it everywhere like you're some amazing pink disco lighthouse. I know it sounds corny, but you will be *shocked* at how immediate the response will be. Men will flock to you. And so will women and children.

If I could sum up this whole Feminine principle thing in one word, it would be to "soften." You do not need to protect yourself or defend yourself anymore. I know this is a radical thing to say.

Most people walk around believing that they need to protect themselves against getting hurt. But if you fully inhabit your Feminine, you will stop doing this.

You can now take this risk for a couple of reasons. First, if you are very self-loving and only get into deep sexual relationships with men you already know are committed to you wholeheartedly, you won't need to protect yourself in the same way you have been. You will know your man loves you and has your back, because you have established that *before* getting all bonded to him. It's not that he will never hurt you—he will—but it won't be coming from a place of callous disregard because he is only in a casual relationship with you.

Even more important, though, is that when you are cultivating your Feminine in a really conscious way, you are practicing your connection to the intangible and the unseen—the source. We'll talk more about the source in Chapter 10, but what this means here is that, actually, *you can never really be hurt.* Nobody can. Because there is a place inside each person—inside you—that is always safe no matter what. Not because it's walled off from the world but because it's *beyond* this world—a place of endless love that, when you're deep in your Feminine, you are aware of. This is the thing you're grounding yourself in, and it's why you can be a loving presence in the lives of your man, your children, and everyone else around you—even when the toilet's backed up and there's nothing in the fridge for dinner. Because you're *connected* to something bigger.

You might think everything I'm saying is pretty out there, but this place I'm talking about—you already have it. It's in you. It's just that our unique gifts—our intuition, our feeling-centered world, our relational abilities, and our abilities to *attract* what we need, see the intangible, and be a source of life—aren't valued by the world the same way society values rocket science, banking, field goals, or, in general, the male way of being in the world. In the technological age a lot of us women have abandoned the Feminine aspects of our being. Not on purpose. It's more that we have forgotten what they are, how they function in relationships, and why we need them—in part because there was no one above us to pass down the collective wisdom. Just like I had to buy a book to figure out how to nurse my baby.

It's time now to get it back because without it, our relationships are lacking a crucial ingredient necessary for success. The cool thing is that as you develop this ingredient in yourself and bring it to your relationships with men, you are also bringing it into the world. A man who is encountering, living with, and/or loving a woman who is deeply aware of and grounded in her Feminine is, simply put, a better, more aware, more grounded man.

Why Valerie's Not Married

My friend Valerie has no idea that being too deep in her Masculine is causing problems in her dating life. It's not that she has a great job in sales at a radio station and earns lots of money. And it's not because she loves sports, wears pants, climbs mountains, has short hair, or whatever else might fall into a traditional definition of what constitutes masculinity. Those things might be dude-like, but they're not necessarily going to affect Valerie's relationships with men.

The reason I say Valerie is in her Masculine is that she has no real sense of *letting a man come to her*. She does not see herself as a force of attraction. She sees herself as a force of getting shit done. Of identifying what she wants and going after it. And she takes this into the dating world. When Valerie walks into a party, she scans the room to see which guys look interesting to her. When she sees one, she often doesn't hesitate to walk right up and start a conversation with him. She's given guys her phone number, and when they don't use it, she's called, texted, or emailed them. Sometimes they go out with her, and sometimes they have sex with her. She considers these dates successes.

I don't! This style of relationship might be fine for a chick who is interested in having fun and amusing sex for a while, but it is *not* the way to get into a lifetime commitment. Valerie's going to need to cultivate her Feminine for that. As my TV agent might say, she will have to let the game come to her. But Valerie insists it's okay for women to call men—she says gender roles are stupid, and she doesn't want to "play games." In her mind, women fought for the right to be equal, and that means acting just like men in every area of life. What Valerie doesn't seem to realize is that in more than a decade of dating "equally," she is in a long-term relationship with exactly *none* of the men she has pursued. (I know there are exceptions to this, but like I said, chances are that if you're reading this book, you're not one of them.)

For a significant majority of men, what Valerie is doing, the way she behaves with them, is not attractive. And by attractive, I'm not talking about whether Valerie has a nice face and figure (she does). What I mean is, if there are millions of particles out there whizzing around, which ones, if any, are going to stick to Valerie?

Let me try another metaphor. A relationship is almost like the set of batteries in, say, a vibrator. There's a plus side (Masculine) and a minus side (Feminine). In order for the thing to start buzzing, you have to have the pluses touching the minuses. Two pluses and nothing happens. Two minuses and nothing happens. The different kinds of energy have to be lined up with their opposites if you want the thing to turn on. And it can't turn *you* on if *it's* not turned on first.

You see, Valerie is "plussing" her relationships to death.

Notes from My Life as a Wife, Not-So-Successful Dater, and Mother

When I started out as a wife, I was very naturally in my Feminine. Why? Because I was only nineteen. I was still swirling around like the ocean (water is a powerful symbol of yin), wondering what I was going to do with my life. It isn't surprising that I attracted the kind of masculine guy who was my first husband. He had just joined a Fortune 500 company and was climbing the ladder (hierarchies are a dude thing) as fast as he could. He no doubt liked the idea that I was someone he could take care of, and no doubt that made him feel powerful, like a man. Yes, that's a simple definition of a man—but at a core level, it's a definition many people are working with. Particularly men.

Ten years later, I had become a lot more powerful in the world. I'd divorced the first husband at twenty-two, earned a college degree, moved all over the country, made some money, and established a halfway-awesome career in TV news. I was doing great, except for one thing: after being in relationships virtually nonstop since I was fifteen, suddenly I was having a hard time attracting anyone—just at the time I was ready to settle down and have a baby. I had no idea why.

All I knew is that girls that I considered wispy or even lame seemed to be getting a lot more action than I was. And it made me angry. I wanted to feel superior to these girls—after all, what were *they* accomplishing?—but it was hard since they seemed to be so much more successful with men than I was. And as much as I hated to admit it, success with men was important to me. I wanted to be wanted.

Around this time I started studying the I Ching and the sacred Feminine and I began to see what I was missing. It's not that I needed to become more of a waif, or make myself "less" in any way; it's that I needed to get grounded. I needed to develop my Feminine.

At first I *hated* this idea. After all, I considered myself a feminist, even if by the mid-1990s I wasn't quite sure exactly what that meant anymore. But I also knew that what I was doing absolutely wasn't working. Still, I wasn't about to do what I perceived as "giving in." I persisted in this damned-if-I-do-damned-if-I-don't behavior for a few more years.

Then I had the great good fortune to get knocked up by a very good guy I had started dating, and nine months later I gave birth to a beautiful baby boy. And in the process of forced surrender known as mothering, I got my first deep acquaintance with what it really means to step into Feminine power.

Motherhood forced me to learn how to let go of goals, plans, and getting my way. I stepped into a world not of schedules but of *cycles:* feeding, sleeping, waking, and playing. I had to dial into a whole other side of myself: the side that intuitively understands things, the side that can hear a baby breathing in the other room, the side that can make a kick-ass snack plate. I started to find a creative center inside myself—I joined a band, started writing music, planted a beautiful garden, and learned how to keep my house clean. All things I really didn't care about when I was a Masculine cute-outfit-wearing worker chick.

The big shocker came when, a few years later, I found myself single again, but this time things were different. Suddenly a ton of guys wanted to date me. How come?

Make Them Want to Be a Better Man

My friend Lucia had an interesting dating issue the other day that made me think about being grounded in the Feminine. She was set up on a blind date with a very eligible, handsome, successful businessman—the kind of guy who has women at "I was a poetry major." Making millions *and* you're sensitive? Let's start picking out dresses!

But this guy also did something very uncool. By email he and Lucia established a probable date for Tuesday (a week away), and then she never heard another word from him until 12:30 a.m. on Tuesday night (technically Wednesday morning). Poetry Man said (poetically, of course) that he'd had an important dinner with colleagues and could they have drinks tomorrow night (technically tonight) instead?

Lucia wanted to know what I thought she should do. I sent her the following email:

Dear Lucia:

First of all, *this is lame.* He knows Tuesday was the plan—that's why he has an excuse and he's emailing you that night. So why beat around the bush? I would be *perfectly honest* with him. If I felt intuitively that there was really something to this guy, I would say yes to the drink and once there I would be completely up front:

You: I almost didn't come to drinks with you tonight. *(Smile)*
Him: Really? Why?

You: Because you did that lame thing by emailing me the night we were supposed to go out at 12:30 a.m. and asking me for a drink the next night. Technically the same night.

Him: (Speechless)

You: Normally I wouldn't even reply, but you were a poetry major, and I felt like maybe there might be something here, so . . . I'm giving you another chance. But . . . *(smile)* I just want you to know right up front, that whole thing is *so* not how I roll. *(Wink, smile)*

One of two things will happen. Either (1) he will get it, and if he really thinks you're his woman, he'll shape up and never do it again. Or (2) he will never call you again. Either way, you win. I am highly doubtful that he would (3) keep dating you and acting like a cad, but some super-entitled dudes would. And a big businessman might easily fall into that group! Just remember to love yourself more than you love him.

xoxo

Tracy

We exchanged sixteen emails in all, and I told Lucia that right here was where this guy was going to find out whether she would allow him to be out of integrity. If she would, he'd know he could slack for the rest of the relationship. If she wouldn't, he'd have to either go big—raise his game—or go home.

I'm a firm believer that men *really want* a woman who is

going to force them to raise their game. That's why Jack Nicholson won an Oscar for telling Helen Hunt she made him want to be a better man in *As Good as It Gets*. Because there's something in the Feminine that raises a man up—which we all intuitively understand.

As for Lucia, she let the guy go without ever doing the drinks date. Strong lady.

Some Relevant Stuff About Men

I hadn't really gotten any better-looking, and since I was now a mom, I also had an unruly three-year-old in tow and a vadge with a few thousand more miles on it. So why did men suddenly find me attractive when before I couldn't seem to get chlamydia if I tried? What had changed?

To make a long story short, I had.

Now I could not only make a snack plate, but actually *tune in* to another person—for instance, a man. I could deal with someone who wasn't focused on me, someone who—this was an especially big deal—possibly wasn't even making me happy. Like, someone who was having a temper tantrum, or needed dinner, or used hand gestures to communicate. Please understand what I mean here. I'm not saying men are children (although even if I were, that wouldn't be a bad thing; *people* are children, for goodness' sake). What I'm saying is that being a woman who can handle her own feelings around another human being who is at times very unreasonable is a major requirement for building a marriage. And before I developed my Feminine, I didn't know how to do that.

This led me to my big epiphany about men: *they need us.*

Oh, I know that the popular culture insists that what men *really* want is to have sex with a new woman every night. And at one level—the animal level, I guess—that might be true. (I love being an animal as much as the next person, so I don't think this is all bad.) But then my question is, why don't they? Why would any guy get married, *ever*? Especially now. In the twenty-first century, no one *has* to get married.

I think the answer is that there's something men want *even more* than they want sex with a new woman every night. Something they need. And that is a really solid source of Feminine energy in their lives that will help ground them emotionally and spiritually and help them expand in the world. (Okay, not all of them. George Clooney is obviously fine with a new thirtysomething lady friend every couple of years or so.) And unless they have some other source of Feminine in their lives—like, if they are surfers and spend a lot of time in the ocean, or they are getting their nurturing from a creative pursuit, like being in a band—the vast majority of men are going to be getting that from their woman.

This plays out on the biological level as well. If a guy spills his, um, seed on the ground, nothing happens. It's just a bunch of stuff. But if he deposits it into some nice, luscious Feminine—well, babies happen. The guy's genes get to make it into the next generation. The same thing is true in terms of a man's work, whatever it is that he is trying to bring into the world. With a great relationship, a man plugs into the fertile Feminine and becomes capable of achieving more than he could accomplish on his own. This is the basic meaning behind the saying "Behind every great man is a great woman."

The question you have now is, how do you become one of those women with the big Feminine-energy battery?

How You're Going to Have to Change

Well, you don't have to become a mother, like I did—though that's one way to cultivate your Feminine. What you're really trying to do is to flip your battery over from the plus to the minus for at least some part of every day. Ideally, you will learn to go back and forth from the Masculine to the Feminine, depending on which energy is required in a given situation. Like being able to write with either hand.

Here are three really simple ways you can start shifting your perception about yourself more toward the feminine.

1. *You're a force of attraction.* You want to begin experiencing yourself as a force of attraction. Start by seeing where you are already attracting people and ideas and things. For example, when you're at lunch today, do an experiment. Become aware of yourself as you stand in line, take a seat, and eat. See who looks at you. Who is noticing your energy and is *attracted* to it? When you feel yourself attracting someone—male or female, old or young, even dogs and babies—smile! Affirm the fact that you are an attractive being. Enjoy the feeling. Remember, Feminine *feels.* It operates on the level of emotion and sensation.

2. *You're a prize.* As you're starting to really feel your attraction energy field, begin to think of yourself as a *prize.* Because you are! You have what every man on the planet needs in order to fulfill his two ambitions: passing along his genes and building things in the world. You need to start seeing yourself as the source of this really powerful energy. This energy is something that you are building—"charging up," if you will—as you continue to develop your Feminine. This whole prize thing also sets you up to take a brand new approach to men from now on. And that is . . .

3. *Let the game come to you.* In biological terms, you are the egg. The egg—like Eminem in that rap movie based on his life—only gets one shot, so it better be good. This is why the egg has to be super picky about who it allows in. Of all the sperm that are trying to get to you, the egg only wants the very best "man" to do the job.

The woman grounded in her Feminine understands that her investment in her egg is *way, way, way, way, way* bigger than the man's investment in his sperm. Guys are sperm factories: they're pumping out fifty-six gazillion of those suckers every day. You have one egg a month, and if you let someone fertilize it, that's gonna be eighteen-plus years of your life that you invest in that egg. Of *course* you need to be selective.

This is why I want Valerie to stop running around acting like the sperm are the prize. Sperm are cheap. *Eggs* are the prize! You (and Valerie) do not need to know if a guy is willing to fuck you, i.e., donate his sperm. The answer is surely going to be yes! What you need to know is, *will that guy send your egg to college?* And if a guy hasn't even bothered to call you or to walk across the room to talk to you, you can be pretty sure the answer to that question is a big fat no.

Which is why, from now on, you do not need to make it easy for a man to date you. I promise you that a man who has been hit over the head with an intuitive understanding that you are what he needs—the source of Feminine energy he needs—will move a mountain and put up with tons of your bullshit to be with you. Because that's how men are—once they think they want something, they are not easily dissuaded.

Let me say this, too: men feel *empowered*—in a good way—by

a woman who is grounded in her Feminine. It's not just about attracting him. It's also about the way you relate to him once you're in the relationship. The Feminine sets the tone in a household. When I'm in healthy touch with my Feminine—which for me means cultivating my relationship to the earth, to nurturing, to

Don't Take His Card

When a guy gives me his number and tells me to call him, I shake my head and smile sweetly. "Oh, I don't call men," I say, point-blank. This never fails to grab their attention. They usually tilt their heads and look at me. Because they realize there is something different going on here. Something they're not used to.

I also think they instantly become *more attracted to me.* Not necessarily sexually—it's more that a guy is forced to "lean in" to find out why I'm telling him I have no intention of calling him. Ever. It's true that men like a challenge, and when you tell them that they're going to have to *do something* in order to even be considered, they immediately get curious. A guy might not be used to dealing with a woman who is approaching dating from this standpoint, but they almost all respond to it.

This is the yin/yang of it all. When you're in your Feminine, a guy will either move into his Masculine or get confused and leave. And if he leaves, yay. Because you do not want to spend the rest of your relationship with a guy who is doing the metaphorical equivalent of handing you his card and asking you to call him.

creating beauty, and to expressing emotions—everyone in my home, my surroundings, is more grounded, too.

Like the folk wisdom says: "A happy wife is a happy life."

Spiritual Stuff That Will Help You Change

All this Feminine stuff sounds fun, right? Dudes hit you up for your phone number, call you, and beg you to commit—what could suck about that? Well, it's not quite that simple. Because, from a spiritual standpoint at least, it's all about *receiving.* Another way to say this is *allowing.* Which sounds good until you realize that, when it comes to dating, it means you are going to have to learn a whole new way of doing business.

When you've been dating a guy for a month and it's going really well but he doesn't call you or text you for one or (God forbid) two days at a time, your mind will start thinking up some premise for getting in touch. If you've been in your Masculine your whole life, it will seem odd not to take action. After all, you know how to make things happen! But resist this temptation. Remind yourself that you only need to know one thing: *how much does he want you?* Enough to pay for your egg's wedding?

So here's what your Feminine looks like in practice. When you meet a man, you are going to have to see if he likes you. You'll know if he likes you because he will try to see you and be in your presence. Remember, he wants to soak up your energy! He might be *slightly* zigzaggy at first, but generally speaking, if he likes you, he will approach you in a straight line. And if he does, you'll practice receiving him—his attention, his ideas, his beingness. If you've been doing your Masculine all this time, you are going to want to direct him around: point out that parking spot over there, give him suggestions about his career or insights you have about his childhood. Rather than jumping into all that, stay on the receiver side of the seesaw. Watch what happens! The man will definitely reveal a side of himself that you have not been seeing on your other dates.

When you're dating a guy you really like, opportunities to stay in your Feminine will be coming at you fast and furious. Because in a way, the whole dating <u>thing</u> is about how grounded you are in your Feminine. You will have to kick the habit of trying to exert all kinds of control over outcomes (but only when it comes to your intimate relationships—you can still be as powerful as you want at work). If it feels like a test, that's because it is—a test to see whether you can love yourself more than you can love him, no matter what's going on. A key skill for partnership.

At the same time you're busy building this key partnership skill, you want to be watching this man to see if you like how he does life. Because if you marry him, that's going to be *your* life. Like my hairdresser friend said, *men do not change.* Not really. They might improve a little, or even a lot, but if a guy is a Labrador retriever, the only thing marriage can do is make him a better Labrador retriever. (Or possibly a worse one.) He'll never turn into, say, a Doberman pinscher.

As you practice all this allowing/receiving during dating, you're going to notice an exquisite new sensation in your body called *being vulnerable.* This feeling doesn't present itself as good, at least not at first. It feels like you could get really hurt by a guy, mostly because you can. If you're not doing anything to protect yourself, like putting up walls, being sarcastic, or jumping into sex right away (because sex feels powerful and oftentimes ends up reducing the anxiety of being vulnerable in the relationship), you might very well feel absolutely terrible. There may be anxiety and tears and a really intense desire to flee the relationship.

Don't worry! This is a good sign. *This is the fear of intimacy that you have had all along.* It's part of why you never wanted to be in your Feminine in the first place—because it's challenging to be vulnerable. But I can assure you that you will get used to it, and as you do, you will discover this whole new type of power.

The power comes from knowing that the guy who is with you is with you because he loves you, and because he wants to be with you. When you're relaxed into your Feminine principle, when you're not trying to "get" anything from a man, the Masculine gets to *choose you.* You're not crossing the line to hunt him down and kill him, and he can feel it. This is the spiritual essence of commitment: when a person chooses to be in a relationship.

Because you are the prize.

What Your Next Boyfriend Will Be So Happy You Now Know

Let's summarize what we've covered in Chapter 9:

- *You're acting like a dude.* Of course it's fine to make a lot of money or love the Cardinals. But when it comes to dating, begin to see yourself as a force of attraction.
- *You are the prize.* You don't need to know if a man is willing to have sex with you. You need to know if he is willing to cross a room, ask for your number, and then use it. If he isn't, he's not your man. Move on.
- *It's not about being "girly."* Being in your well-developed Feminine is not about wearing pink or being less of a person.

It's about being grounded in a deep knowledge of cycles, of intuition, of the *other* kind of creative power. It's already in there; it just needs to be developed.

- ***Practice being receptive.*** Love yourself, and your life, more than you love him. Trust that you will get what you need.
- ***Be vulnerable.*** Relating from your Feminine principle can be frightening. You will be tempted to move into your Masculine as a defense. Don't! You don't need to protect yourself against the man who wants to build a future with you; you want to *join* with him.

10. You're Godless

Or, If You Could Change on Your Own,
You Already Would Have

1. Is there a part of you that has grown cynical about the odds of finding love?
2. Is there another part of you that, deep down, believes there's something even more powerful than the odds?
3. Are you willing to start putting that belief into practice?

REMEMBER WHEN I SAID this was going to be a spiritual book? Well, we're there.

This is the point where I suggest the totally crazy thing that might cause you to throw this book across the room. Or, I hope, the totally crazy thing that is going to bring everything we've been talking about in these chapters together, take this whole journey you're on to the next level, and ultimately bring you the relationship—to yourself, to men, to *life*—that you want. So what's the totally crazy thing?

I want you to get a god. (With a little *g*.)

Okay, I know god is off-limits for a lot of people, but what I mean by god is something so elastic and so personal that pretty much everyone—even the super-stubborn atheist lady—can find one that fits. Like one of those tube dresses they sell on late-night TV for $29.99 that you can make into a halter, or a bandeau, or a skirt. Whatever you need your version of god to do, it can do.

One thing I can assure you: I don't mean a bearded dude in the sky who is watching you all the time and is going to give you a Mercedes and a husband if you're good and punish you if you're bad. That wouldn't be god, that would be Santa Claus. Nor does the thing I'm talking about belong to any particular belief system—it's not Mormon, or Hindu, or Catholic, or Buddhist, or Scientologist. (Unless, of course, you want it to be.) Maybe you don't like the religion you were raised with, or maybe you *love* your religion and you think it's awesome, the only one for you. Either way, this thing can include you. The only reason I call it god in the first place is because that's a word that we all sort of know the meaning of.

A better term might be "spirit." It's the thing that makes you who you are—totally unique. Some people call it Creative Intelligence. In *Star Wars* they call it the Force. Others think of it as the Higher Self. In Eastern philosophy, it's known as the Tao (the Way). Shoot, you could call it Jessica! But whatever you name it, it's the power behind the oceans, gravity, chocolate, and the Beatles. It's the thing that beats your heart.

Spirit belongs to every denomination and no denomination, and it is found everywhere. It's the engine that not only brings you the kind of relationship that you are really looking for but also drives it. As I've said, there really is no perfect person out there. What *is* out there is someone you are going to walk a path with, someone who will walk a path with you. How will you know who that someone is? What should that someone be like? What if that someone has flaws, big ones, that make you scared to commit? (You can be sure that this will be the case. After all, you're not perfect, right? So he won't be, either.) Why would you risk giving up your great rent-controlled apartment for an ordinary guy who will not only see all your flaws but also have the power to leave you? None of it makes sense.

Unless you decide to make this whole relationship *thing* about something way bigger.

What It's Really About

Which brings us to what this whole book is about, really: *love*. Love is the big thing we human beings get to learn here on Earth, if we decide to really go for it in life and see what's beyond the cash and prizes. To love someone is to accept them as flawed. To marry them is to give them the gift of being loved despite those flaws. That includes you.

Love means possibilities, and I don't mean that in a Hallmark way. I mean it for real. Spirit is the solution for your (supposed) single-lady "problem": whether it's that there aren't enough men, or that you need to "settle" for a man, or even that you're just a little bit slutty. Spirit makes it possible to accomplish (after Chapter 9 you now know the more precise word is "attract") things that appear to be impossible, unlikely, or in defiant opposition to any sort of reasonable odds, at least as far as the demographers, the advertising executives, or even the evolutionary biologists are concerned. They'll tell you that to find a mate you need to be just the right age, or have just the right beauty, or have the right number of eggs remaining. But spirit says something else.

Spirit says that those things might be factual, but they're not *true.* There's a difference. When spirit gets involved in your love life, there are no more odds. There are no more demographics. There are only two people on a spiritual assignment. And spirit will move a mountain and make the impossible possible in order to make it happen. You know, deep down, in your deepest heart that this is so. Everyone knows it—it's why we could never tire of love stories. A love story is just a reminder that the impossible and the unlikely *can* and *do* happen, all the time. I want you to commit to that knowledge right now, because it's your commitment that brings it into being.

Which takes us to the other thing this whole book is about, really: *transformation.* Sorry for the woo-woo word, but it's really the right one for what I'm talking about. Transformation is the process in which you go from what and how you are now—and maybe what and how you've been your whole life—to being some *new* way, the way you want to be, the way that will lead to the life you want. Doesn't that sound awesome?

Except the thing about transformation is this: you can't just *make* it happen. Okay, wait, sometimes you can—on the purely physical level. If you do four hundred sit-ups and push-ups and biceps curls every day for a month, your body will start to look all muscley. But just try that with, say, acting like a bitch, or being super jealous, or only wanting to date guys who are 10s. Your push-ups are no good here. That's because willpower works when it works, but when it doesn't it doesn't. And when it doesn't, what is a sister to do?

This is where spirit comes in. There is something about culti-vating and tapping into a sense of a power bigger than anything down here on earth—anything limited to your five senses—that can bring about change where everything else has failed. It is the same power that will bring your perfect relationship into existence, and your babies—however they get here.

Then there's the *other* other thing you get from a god—*meanings.* Meanings give your life and what happens in it a sense of significance or importance. Some people don't need meanings. To them, meanings feel unnecessary, or even undesirable in an opiate-of-the-masses kind of way. Maybe you're one of these people. (You know if you are.) Most of my philosophy-major friends are among these people. In their world, things are totally random, and that's fine with them. Not me. I like it when things mean something. For example, in my world, when you sat down next to me at the DMV, it was because there was something trying to happen in my life and it needed you to get the ball rolling. Suddenly you were there for a reason. And that reason is part of what we are going to spend our relationship working on. It might even keep us together somehow.

That's because when you put meaning on something random, it becomes a story, and as you know by now, I love stories. I believe every good relationship needs one. As I said earlier, stories are how human beings organize their experience. This is super important when it comes to relationships. Without a story, it can be a lot harder to know why you're bothering to put up with some guy's bullshit—not abusive bullshit, just normal, everyday bullshit—and I can be pretty sure that sometime in the next forty-five years of marriage you are going to be asking yourself why you are putting up with this guy's bullshit.

The other thing about meanings is that you're probably making them whether you want to or not. Very few people—outside maybe of some of the crazies who used to write letters to the news anchors back when I worked in TV news—believe *everything* is random. If you really press most people, even the philosophy majors, they'll usually admit that at least once something happened in their lives that made them feel like there's a bigger force going on in life—something beyond what can be perceived with the five senses, maybe even beyond what can be measured with the most powerful microscope, telescope, or math formula. Not everything can be explained, least of all marriage.

Which is why—between love, transformation, and meanings—developing a sense of the spiritual is the final piece of the puzzle toward becoming ready for marriage.

Notes from My Life as a Serious Fixer-Upper

For the first four or so decades of my life, I was like a house that was—and this is putting it charitably—a fixer-upper. A serious fixer-upper. Underneath all the layers of bad wallpaper and stained carpeting, you could see that there was something good there. But getting down to it was not going to be easy.

What's more, remodeling my life, my *self*, seemed hugely overwhelming. At that point in my spiritual development, if I couldn't *see* how something was going to happen, I wouldn't believe that it could. It's not like I had Ty Pennington and a team of guys ready to come in and do an episode of *Extreme Makeover Home Edition*. To me, seeing was believing. If I couldn't see it, I couldn't believe it.

Turns out I had everything exactly backward. In fact, *believing is seeing*. Now, I don't mean to go all *The Secret* on you, but you really do have to believe something before you can see it. For example, pretend you're going to invent something. Like, I don't know, a cell phone. Before you can get down to putting all the little widgets and doohickeys together, first you have to imagine talking on the phone while walking around the block, and then you have to believe *that it could, in some universe, be possible to do such a thing,* even though you've spent your whole life tethered to a tightly coiled springy cord that gets all tangled up in your legs while you pace around your kitchen.

Only once you've committed to those two ideas could you (or is it *would* you?) start pulling together widgets and doohickeys. And even then it might've taken *years* to work your way through the interim versions—like the cordless phone that would only go as far as the edge of the front yard.

This was true of my own personal evolution, too—from the landline where I started, through all the cordless-phone relationships, to where I am now, a place of flourishing. And—whether I am in a relationship or not—a place of self-love.

Why Angie's Not Married

My life used to look a little more like that of Angie—a pretty good example of a girl with no god. Actually, it's not that she has no god. It's that the god she has *sucks*. Here's how you identify someone's god: it's the person, place, or thing they turn to with the problems in their life. It's the thing that, for them, makes everything okay again. It's the thing they are compulsive about, but usually they don't call it that—they just think they like it a lot. It's the thing they definitely don't want to go without.

For Angie, that thing is *relationships*. When Angie's not with a guy (pretty much any guy will do) she feels restless and unhappy. In a relationship, even a bad one, her whole life feels better. She can handle a rough day at work knowing she has a man to turn to; like a glass of wine at the end of the day, a partner (even one who's not really committed, or obviously wrong for her) calms her down and restores her vitality. Not only that, but when Angie's in a relationship (even if it's a messy one), some of her worst behaviors lessen or even disappear altogether—she stops drinking so much, and her compulsive cleaning is nowhere in evidence. She always says men are good for her, and in some ways that's true. At least temporarily.

But she's thirty-four, and it's beginning to wear thin—for her and for them. Because a relationship is so key to Angie feeling good about herself, she's always employed a sort of Ferris wheel approach to men: while one guy is up at the top checking out the view, she is busy loading backups into the seats down at the bottom. These days, however, there seem to be fewer men who are willing to take a spin with Angie, and it's really affecting her. Life feels flat and boring. She's looked into going on antidepressants. It's becoming clear that for Angie, men are more than just a partner—they're more like a higher power. They do for Angie what she can't seem to do on her own, which is reveal the most beautiful version of her walls, her floors, her windows—her *self*.

That's how you know men are Angie's god. They have the power to make her feel better, more alive, more whole. Admitting that this is a problem is tough, since pretty much everything in our culture tells us love will make us feel whole, even when we aren't. And, from a chemical perspective, that is true: love comes with some very powerful hormones and things that make everyone feel all brand-new. The difference is, while most people can let that awesome phase pass and settle into the next part of the relationship, Angie has to leave to go find some more awesome.

And for Angie, awesome is a new man.

Some Relevant Stuff About Men

Men don't really like being a girl's higher power. It makes them feel squeamish, and for good reason. For one thing, on an intuitive level, guys know that if you are willing to make *them* your higher power, you will be just as willing to replace them with the next fabulous guy who comes along. They also understand that it's sort of mentally unstable to make another human being, a mere mortal, your source—or at least it does once your age no longer ends with the word "teen." And last but not least, guys know that when you make them your source, you will tend to do what people do for a higher power: *absolutely anything.* And that is truly frightening.

No guy wants to be with a woman who will do *anything* to be with him, because in practice "anything" usually means some version of being a sobbing mess on his doorstep or accidentally moving into the apartment next door after he breaks things off. It might also mean performing drastic acts of anything, like getting knocked up or forwarding the emails he sent you to his boss or his mom. And no man wants that. What men want is to trust you. And if you can't live without a man, you are going to be about as trustworthy as a Miss America contestant in the interview portion of the competition.

What makes you trustworthy is when you have a sense of some kind of spirit-god-Yahweh thing *that isn't your man.* In Chapter 9's discussion on the Feminine, we talked about how a man plugs into your Feminine power (literally and figuratively) in order to expand himself into the world. That power comes from your connection with your source. It can't come from him.

Having your own source also changes the pH level in a relationship, in three really important ways. (1) A guy knows that you are going to be okay with or without him. Which means (2) he knows he better be good to you because you will have no problem leaving his lame ass if he's not. But perhaps most important, (3) the bigger your source, the bigger he will be able to become in partnership with you.

This is the intangible "thing" that causes a man to choose a particular woman as his life partner. Not how cute you are, or that you're from the right family, or that you went to the right school. Those are all nice, but they are not deal makers in a really good marriage. It's when a man knows that within a given relationship he is going to be able to expand into the person he knows he can be that *he is moved to commit.* And when *you* have some kind of higher power, you are much more likely to be in a place where that can happen.

How You're Going to Have to Change

For nine chapters we've been talking about ways that you have to change. And now we've reach a sort of circular question. How do you change . . . so that you *can* change? We've already established that if you could just snap your fingers and make it happen, you would have already done so. If people could do that, there would be no wish fulfillment in a show like *Bewitched.* We wouldn't find it interesting that there's a pretty blond lady living right next door who can wiggle her nose and summon a new outfit or a clean house, or, if it's us, the ability to suddenly be a lot nicer than we feel, or stop having sex with guys who don't love us. Behaviors we've been doing for years, possibly decades.

But the fact of the matter is that, most of the time, we human beings are stuck the way we are until somehow, some way, some *thing* allows transformation to happen. And what I am suggesting is, that the *thing* that allows the transformation to happen is what I am going to call—just for simplicity's sake—god. Or, more precisely, a *godspiritwhatchamacallit.*

So where do you get one of those? Well, the good news is, you can make one yourself. For free. Starting right now. The details of this source are up to you—it's like Build-A-Bear, you can decorate it whatever way you want. You decide how to conceptualize it, what it feels like, what qualities it has, and what it can do for you. The only caveat is that you have to make sure you're working with the prescription-strength version, not the over-the-counter stuff. You have to understand a source that has enough power to bring about the transformation. Which is not really that hard.

Here are a few qualities I really like in a spirit thing. Feel free to borrow any of these or make up some of your own:

1. *Super nice.* Grandma nice. Never punishes or tries to teach me painful lessons. Never snaps at me, and I don't have to be particularly careful—I can take off my seat belt and move around the cabin of life. Bump into stuff, too.

2. *Really powerful.* Can remove any stain, no matter how long it has been there. Can move inner (and outer) boulders blocking my progress even if they're the size of Connecticut.

3. *Compassionate.* Thinks I'm adorable even when I'm seriously fucking up. Always gives me another chance. Never says judgy things, even when we both knew full well that my latest debacle was going to turn into, well, a debacle.

4. *Knows everyone.* Can make the craziest introductions/ coincidences happen. Can make a cute guy I met last week show up next Tuesday in a completely other part of town.

5. *Healing.* Like that cheerleader on the TV show *Heroes*. Except it might take longer—time I use to develop patience, or other aspects of myself that need developing.

6. *Is right where you are now.* Even at the awful work event I absolutely have to go to. Even in Vegas. Most important: my source never tells me that if only I can just get somewhere other than where I am now, help will be on the way. It's always right here, right now.

7. *Loving and forgiving.* Wants what's best for me, even if that's hard to see at the time. Doesn't hold grudges.

8. *Is handling shit.* You know how they can send up a spaceship and it arrives at Mars twelve years later exactly on schedule? That's because my god is *predictable.* Things go according to a really tight schedule, which I like to think of as a plan that includes my life.

9. *Is like Twyla Tharp.* My spirit thing is a genius choreographer. The waves move with the tides, which move with the moon, which moves with the sun. And all while I'm sitting here watching *Seinfeld* reruns, eating Tofutti Cuties.

Once you've got a Big Something, start getting to know it. How do you do that? Well, first of all, you begin to see it everywhere. Seeing it everywhere looks like this: when you've got a song stuck in your head, then turn on the radio and there it is. When for some reason you're thinking about your sixth-grade best friend, then go on Facebook and she's friended you. Or when you were just talking about Peru, then the guy you go out on a date with that night chooses a Peruvian restaurant. You begin to look for, and see, the *interconnectedness* of everything. Because the Big Something is about connection.

I'm not saying you should live in a magical world where you think all coincidences are evidence of aliens, or you read your fortune in the license plate of the car ahead of you, or that you believe that you're communicating telepathically with the cute guy in Purchasing. You have to stay grounded!

But when I began to really look and, especially, *feel* my way around things that seemed coincidental, I realized that these so-called coincidences are happening all day long. After a while, it became obvious—to me, at least—that the odds are stacked so high against having four "coincidences" taking place in one thirty-six-hour period that maybe they weren't actually coincidences after all.

Which led me to view life in a whole different way. For one thing, I started asking a new question: What if whatever was happening to me wasn't random? Then how would I perceive it? Asking myself this, especially around dating situations, forced me to go deeper into things. For example, if I assume that a guy isn't calling me back because it's part of the interconnectedness, and I don't make it about there being something wrong with me, suddenly it is a lot easier to accept. Like I said earlier, when there's a bigger order in your universe, you know for sure your real man can never get away. If he's yours, you'll know it, because he'll be sitting in therapy with you at eight-thirty on a Monday morning, or taking out your garbage without being asked.

Once you get acquainted with your big something, the next thing that happens is that you *invite* this interconnectedness-spirit-thingy to your life party. Let's say you meet a super-cute guy at a charity fund-raiser. Sure, you ask your friend about him, and maybe you even tell her to do a little reconnaissance. But you don't need to hound her at all, asking her for the next two months if she's had a chance to see if he liked you. You don't even need to check out his page on LinkedIn. Because in addition to making a couple of inquiries about the guy here on the earth plane, you've also gone to your higher power. You've said: *Dear Big Something, if you want me to be with that guy, hook it up!* Then you set it aside and rest in your knowledge that if that guy is your man, you will know, because he will be picking you up and taking you hiking. And if he's not, it doesn't even necessarily mean he's not your man *ever*, but it does mean he's not your man today. And living in today is the only way to be alive.

When you first start practicing this, what might immediately surface is a fear that if you don't do something, *anything*—at the very least get on eHarmony.com—you will not get this guy (or any other guy) and will end up alone. This is where *trust* comes in. Obviously, you don't have the power to make that song play on the radio. You could sing songs and turn the radio on and off all day long, but you couldn't *make* it happen. But somehow the universe does. You know it does because you're seeing the interconnectedness happening all day long. There's no way there can be this whole web of interconnectedness on the planet without you somehow being a part of it. I mean, are you not part of gravity? You know gravity is happening right where you are, so you might as well believe that the interconnectedness is happening for you, too.

There's another word for this: you become *willing*. Willingness is the key to transformation. Why? Because hoping for something can get you up to a door, but willingness opens it. Let's take the example of being married. You would like a wonderful partnership. But you read in a magazine that there are no good men left in your state. Apparently someone has gone door to door and discovered that all the good ones either are married, are gay, or have moved to Puerto Rico. (This is a ridiculous example, but then again, not really, because I seem to read this article every other day.) This is where you are going to have to move into willingness. Are you willing to have your husband materialize anyway—maybe as a result of some miracle-type thing or higher power? I mean, can you allow for the possibility that maybe one guy—your guy— missed his flight to Puerto Rico and got stuck here and is just about to walk through the door to the café you're sitting in right now? And even if you can't believe that for the next few months, are you willing to believe it for the next five minutes?

If not, your other choice—and it is a *choice*—is to give up. You will then close your heart. You protect yourself against disappointment by shutting down to the possibility of ever getting what you want. This is what a lot of single ladies do, and it's why they sometimes come across as hurt or angry. The heart closes and there's a tightness that is palpable—to the person with the closed heart, and to the person she's talking with.

All I want you to know is this: if you're feeling like something will never happen, *it is not proof of anything.* It is only a sign that your willingness has gone behind the clouds and you need to open yourself to the possibility again. And again and again.

Which brings us to the final big, giant point of this book. You ready?

Spiritual Stuff That Will Help You Change

If there is one thing I hope you walk away with from this book, I hope it is this: a marriage is a spiritual path. It is a *practice,* the practice of being loving to yourself and to a man. (And later to your children if you have them, as well as to the other members of your family and your community.)

Your ability to keep opening your heart in the face of

challenges—internal and external—is going to be the basis of your marriage. This life of practice doesn't necessarily start when you say "I do." Some ladies need to learn this in order to *get* a marriage. Some ladies (like me) have to learn it in order to *keep* one. Still other ladies are born knowing it already. (Good for fucking them, right?) It's really only a matter of where and when you start. We all have to start somewhere.

Practice plus *willingness* plus *source* (your highest self) will together resolve every single obstacle in the way of becoming the person that you want to be—and thus pave the way for your life becoming what you know it can be.

One way I visualize bringing all three of these things together is this: I imagine a Mayan ruin. Then I imagine the thing I am trying to let go of. Let's say it's my fear of abandonment—that's a big one for me. I take my abandonment fear and I hold it in my hands—like the Mayans might have taken a big basket of mangoes—and I walk up all the millions of tiny steps on the pyramid that lead up to the place where you leave your offerings to the sun god, or whatever. And though it is super hard for me to let go of that big basket of mangoes—because, in my mind, that fear of abandonment is keeping me safe from people who will hurt me, so it feels like a really big deal to let it go—I am willing to leave it up there, because from here on out, I'm going to let my spirit thing handle my life. All of it.

Now, the only reason I'm willing to do *that* is because I'm forty-seven years old and handling it myself hasn't worked. I have tried—until the wheels fell off. It got me three divorces and a lot of hard knocks. So at last I'm willing to suspend my long experiment in trying to manage my relationship challenges my way, and try something else.

I know you're probably asking how visualizing mangoes and

Mayan ruins is going to change anything (sounds like a whole lotta doing nothing, right?), but I know from experience that once a shift happens internally, transformation *will* happen—and it won't happen until then. It's all about the internal shift. How you get to that internal shift doesn't really matter; you could use anything from spiritual dance to meditation to volunteer work to going to a sweat lodge. That's individual to each person—a sort of Build-A-Honey-Pot that goes with your Build-A-Bear. All I know for sure is, if you continue to commit to the internal shift, it will happen. To paraphrase that baseball movie, if you build it, change will come (though probably not with a young Kevin Costner).

Some people think of god as *love.* That's a really cool definition for transforming yourself because it helps you to soften toward the areas where you are looking to change. For instance, it allows you to think of the reasons you're not married as nothing more than spots in your life that are out of order—like when you're setting a table and the knife is on the wrong side or the spoon is just a little bit askew. These things don't have to be evidence of some huge flaw in you. They're just showing you a place where you need to put something back into order.

You can pretty much say that every single one of the reasons you're not married originates in fear. Fear that you won't get what you need. Fear that you will lose what you have. The thing about love is, it's the antidote to fear. If you simply look upon every area where you now have fear and shine the light of love on it, it will begin to transform.

When you're more focused on love than you are on fear, you're naturally showing up as graceful. You know you're taken care of, so you're not being greedy or shallow. There's no need to lie because you aren't worried about keeping someone in your life who doesn't belong there. You don't even think about that sort of thing anymore. You know that you are supplied, like if you were a daisy in a field—all you do is just turn toward the sun. You're not grasping at anything. It's there, and you're in it.

All that said, there will be challenges along the way on your path to transformation. Challenges that will make it really hard to stay the course. The two biggies are:

1. When you can't seem to change.
2. When you really have changed but you still haven't gotten what you wanted.

Both these apparent problems have the same solution: more practice. Even when it looks like nothing is happening and your mind starts telling you change is never going to come or your life is never going to happen, it is your responsibility to yourself (and your future husband) to keep returning to your vision, *to your source.* Again and again.

And again and again and again.

There will be times when you won't be able to see how it could *ever* happen. (Also called losing faith.) Don't worry about that. What your heart desires is not gone. It's never gone. It's just temporarily hidden from view. Your task is just to keep returning to the *yes.*

Yes about you. Yes about him. Yes about the whole damn world, really.

Now here's the beautiful thing. This process is precisely what you are going to do as a great wife. You are going to stay in the *yes* no matter what comes down the pike in your marriage. In sickness and in health. For richer or for poorer. For better or for worse. You are going to be that Feminine principle, plugged into something higher than the bank account balance, the test results, the hard times, and the full head of hair.

You are going to rock this thing. You are going to be a joy to those around you. You will be a light in their lives. All kinds of good and wonderful things and people will be attracted into your life. And before you know it, you will find that you are about to become someone's wife.

Just like I knew you would be.

What You Know Now

So let's summarize Chapter 10:

- ***You're godless.*** Cultivate a sense of source that can bring about change in you and in your life, even where everything else has failed.
- ***Build your own.*** Your spirit thing can be whatever you want it to be. Give it qualities you want it to have; don't be limited by definitions of god that you've grown up with, or those of other people. This is something really personal. You don't have to defend it to anyone. And know that your definition of spirit can constantly grow and change as you grow and change.
- ***Don't make men your higher power.*** They don't want the job, and besides, they're bad at it.
- ***Become willing.*** It's the key to change. Allowing for the possibility that the unlikely or "impossible" can happen is a choice. Choose it! The only other option is to close your heart. And if you close your heart—even if you just close it to men but keep it open to, say, purse dogs—you will be passing up

what is perhaps life's greatest opportunity to expand as a human being.

- **_Start practicing._** Marriage is a spiritual path. It is the practice of being loving—to yourself and to a man. And it doesn't start when people throw rice all over you and you upload a cute video of your first dance on YouTube. It starts _now_. So go for it!

Epilogue

OF COURSE, I MET A GUY. One month to the day after the "Why You're Not Married" article appeared in The Huffington Post, I'm sitting in a bookstore/coffeehouse tapping away on my computer and he sat down right next to me, wearing a beard and carrying an empty laundry basket. We started chatting. Over the next half hour we covered male bonding hormones, oxytocin, my dad the criminal, his dad the Vietnam vet, my mom the prostitute, and his mom the spiritualist—and after it had become clear that his clothes had probably dried to a crisp and it was time to go, he asked for my phone number. "We have to keep talking," he said. He texted me that night, and the next day we went on a three-hour hike.

We fell in love. We got into a relationship. That was (at the time of this writing) eight months ago. He is shockingly intelligent, is challenging in the best way, and doesn't take any of my crap. A trifecta.

And here's what I found out: *I am everything in this book!* Of course, I knew that already, but it all seemed so much more theoretical when I was single. And I had been single for quite some time.

For the past six months, I have been writing this thing while living this thing. And he has been living it with me, God bless his heart. Because it hasn't been cute every second of the day. Sometimes it's got mascara streaming down its face and hair like a rat's nest. Other times it's sublime—a gorgeous, amazing, remarkable, breathtaking *something* unlike anything I've ever experienced.

In other words, it has been *real.* We're just two people doing life. We've got our hopes, our fears, our dreams, our awesome and our not so awesome. Mostly we've got our willingness to love each other for one more day—right where we are. It's a gift, really.

As for marriage?

At eight months of relationship, it's really too soon to say for sure. But I can say this: we're talking about it.

Acknowledgments

FIRST AND FOREMOST, I want to say how grateful I am to all the women (and men) who have opened their hearts and shared their stories with me. The world changes when one person speaks honestly and another person listens with his or her soul. I can only hope that this book—irreverence and swear words notwithstanding—honors the many conversations I've had over the years in a way that brings a little more love into the world. Thank you for letting me be part of your journey.

Many thanks to my editor, Pamela Cannon—and the whole team at Random House/Ballantine—for making this book such a pleasure to bring into being. You guys are like a great spouse—supportive, encouraging, and always letting me think I'm getting my way.

Thanks also to my team at WME, in particular my book agent, Andy McNicol, for her fantastic instincts. And to Nancy Josephson, Tom Wellington, Kirby Kim, Simon Faber, and Adriana Alberghetti—I am so grateful for your support and representation. You all are right there every time I'm ready to expand, and I can't thank you enough.

Very special thanks go to Arianna Huffington and Roy Sekoff at

The Huffington Post for giving me a place to say what I *really* think. This book would not be what it is without you. Thanks also to Hallie Seegal and Sara Wilson for being such smart and insightful editors.

I must also thank Jill Soloway on multiple counts. 1) For creating Sit 'n Spin, the staged reading series where I performed the original "Why You're Not Married" essay. That night changed my life as a writer. 2) For being a terrific friend and mentor. And 3) for reminding me what this is really all about: serving others. This book would not be here without you, lady.

Thanks also to Carrie Byalick, Molly Kawachi, Victoria Taylor, Natalie Lent, and the whole gang at ID PR for being so kick-ass. I'll just say this: You ladies are pretty much single-handedly making up for my bad childhood.

Major love and gratitude go to my fifteen-year-old son. You are awesome. You inspire me. And like any parent, all I can do is apologize profusely and hope that one day, possibly, with any luck at all, some time after the age of thirty-five, having me for a mom won't have been a total bust.

And lastly, to Luke, my deepest gratitude. I am humbled by your patience, courage, wisdom, and love. You have lived every minute of this book with me, and you stood with me as it took me all the places a book takes a woman deep within. You are a hero! In the process, you have given me the ultimate gift: the opportunity to love more and better. I am thankful beyond words and I love you.

About the Author

TRACY MCMILLAN is a television writer whose credits include *Mad Men, United States of Tara, Life on Mars,* and *Necessary Roughness.* She's the author of the memoir *I Love You and I'm Leaving You Anyway.* She lives in Los Angeles and is the mother of a fifteen-year-old son.

About the Type

This book was set in Bodoni Book, a typeface named after Giambattista Bodoni, an Italian printer and type designer of the late eighteenth and early nineteenth centuries. It is not actually one of Bodoni's fonts but a modern version based on his style and manner and is distinguished by a marked contrast between the thick and thin elements of the letters.